DOCTOR WHO

THE TARDIS HANDBOOK

Steve Tribe

BOOKS

12 13 14 15 16 17 18 19 20

Published in 2010 by BBC Books,
an imprint of Ebury Publishing.
A Random House Group Company

The Random House Group Limited Reg. No. 954009

Addresses for companies within the Random House Group
can be found at www.randomhouse.co.uk

A CIP catalogue record for this book is available
from the British Library.

ISBN 978 1 846 07986 3

MIX
Paper from
responsible sources
FSC® C015829
www.fsc.org

The Random House Group Limited supports the Forest
Stewardship Council® (FSC®), the leading international
forest-certification organisation. Our books carrying
the FSC label are printed on FSC®-certified paper. FSC is
the only forest-certification scheme supported by the
leading environmental organisations, including Greenpeace.
Our paper procurement policy can be found at
www.randomhouse.co.uk/environment

For Lucy

Commissioning editor:
Albert DePetrillo
Creative consultant:
Justin Richards
Editor: **James Goss**
Project editor: **Kari Speers**
Designer: **Paul Lang**
Production: **Phil Spencer**

Printed and bound
in Great Britain by
Printer Trento S.r.l.

To buy books by your favourite
authors and register for offers,
visit **www.rbooks.co.uk**

All 2010 transmission dates are
correct at time of going to press.

BBC Books would like to thank
the following for providing
photographs and for permission
to reproduce copyright material.
While every effort has been
made to trace and acknowledge
all copyright holders, we
would like to apologise should
there have been any errors or
omissions. All images copyright
© BBC, except:
Page 25 (bottom left)
design drawing courtesy
Jan Vincent-Rudzki
Pages 25 (bottom right), 55,
56 and 102 design drawings
courtesy Universal Television

With additional thanks to:
**Lee Binding, Russell T Davies,
Ian Grutchfield, Clayton Hickman,
Steven Moffat, James North,
Glenn Ogden, Nicholas Payne,
Edward Russell, Gary Russell,
Gavin Rymill, Tom Spilsbury,
Robert W. Stewart, David Turbitt
and Jan Vincent-Rudzki. And
special thanks to my incomparable
researcher, Kieran Tribe.**

CONTENTS

INTRODUCTION

Doctor Who began with a police box. As the opening titles of the very first episode faded away, a little after a quarter past five on Saturday 23 November 1963, viewers saw a policeman make his way down a foggy London street and pause at a pair of large gates. The gates swung slowly open to reveal a dark and gloomy junkyard, and there – in amongst the unwanted bric-a-brac and abandoned oddments – stood an ordinary metropolitan police public call box.

Or perhaps not so ordinary. Why on earth would a police box be standing in a junkyard, not on a street corner? And why was it making that strange humming sound?

Minutes later, two schoolteachers were quarrelling with a mysterious old man in the junkyard, convinced that he had abducted one of their pupils and locked her in this oddly situated police box. They forced their way through its doors to discover it was the gateway to whole new worlds and times.

The TARDIS Handbook is an exploration of the Doctor's frankly magnificent time machine, inside and out, through five decades (or 900 years) of adventures, from the history of the police box itself to the designs for the latest incarnation of the TARDIS interior. Everybody knows that the TARDIS is bigger on the inside, that

it's disguised as a police box, and that it can travel through time and space. For almost 50 years, millions of viewers have watched the Doctor, a Time Lord from the planet Gallifrey, journey through the cosmos in this marvellous machine. You probably know that TARDIS is an acronym, and that it stands for Time and Relative Dimension in Space. But if you've ever wondered why the TARDIS looks the way it does, which of its possibly infinite number of rooms have been seen on screen and how production teams over the years have realised them, what you can do with a gravitic anomaliser, or, actually, what is a police box anyway, the answers are in these pages.

But first, let's go back to the Dawn of Time and try to piece together the history of the mighty civilisation that first discovered the principles of time travel and invented the travel capsules known as TARDISes...

THE TIME LORDS
OF GALLIFREY

A t the very centre of the universe, orbiting twin suns at the heart of the constellation of Kasterborous, lay the planet Gallifrey. Its galactic coordinates were ten-zero-eleven-zero-zero by zero-two from Galactic Zero Centre, and it was sometimes known as the Shining World of the Seven Systems. Its endless mountain ranges were slopes of silver-leaved trees and deep red grass, capped with snow that shone in the dual sunlight under burnt-orange skies. In the mountains of Solace and Solitude on the continent of Wild Endeavour, there was a vast glass dome, surrounding and protecting the Citadel of the oldest and most powerful race in the cosmos.

The humanoid Gallifreyans had telepathic and telekinetic capabilities and made scientific advances and discoveries at a ferocious pace. They developed and transcended technologies of space travel, matter transmission, dematerialisation theory and transdimensional engineering during the Old Time, when the universe was less than half its present size, and sought the ability to travel through and gain mastery over time itself. An early development during this period – later known as the Dark Days – was the Time Scoop. This was used to ensnare beings from anywhere and anywhen in the universe and deposit them on Gallifrey in what became known as the Death Zone. Official histories – which were rarely entirely reliable – stated

THE FIVE DOCTORS
by Terrance Dicks
starring Peter Davison,
Jon Pertwee, Patrick
Troughton, Richard
Hurndall, William
Hartnell and Tom
Baker as the Doctor
First UK broadcast:
25/11/1983

that this practice was eventually stamped out by the first President of the Time Lords.

Rassilon was an engineer and architect, later known as the founder of Time Lord society. He directed time-travel research, and he and a solar engineer called Omega developed the living metal Validium and a remote stellar manipulator that could turn a sun into a supernova. Omega used this device to detonate a nearby star, supplying the enormous quantities of energy needed for the

ongoing and soon-to-be successful time-travel experiments. It was a fantastic feat of stellar engineering, but Omega himself was sucked through the resultant black hole into an antimatter universe. The Time Lords were now able to travel through time, but had no idea that the cost of their new freedom was Omega's perpetual imprisonment.

With Omega apparently dead, Rassilon completed the mission, securing the required power source. Shortly afterwards (whether by popular acclaim or political scheming) Rassilon became the first Lord High President of the Time Lords. According to the Book of the Old Time:

Rassilon travelled into the black void with a great fleet. Within the void no light would shine, and nothing of that outer nature continue in being except that which existed within the Sash of Rassilon. Now Rassilon found the Eye of Harmony, which balances all things that they may neither flux, nor wither, nor change their state in any measure. And he caused the Eye to be brought to the world of Gallifrey, wherein he sealed this beneficence with the Great Key. Then the people rejoiced...

The Sash of Rassilon was a protective device that prevented its wearer from being sucked into a black hole (the fate Omega had suffered). The Eye of Harmony was the nucleus of a black hole, which Rassilon stabilised, sealed inside a monolith on Gallifrey with an ebonite rod (the Great Key), and set in an eternally dynamic equation against the mass of the planet Gallifrey.

With Gallifrey's ruling elite now transformed into the Lords of Time, President Rassilon laid down five Great Principles for governing their new realm. These may have formed the basis of the Time Lord Constitution which specified the hierarchy and governance of Gallifrey. The President was at the head of the High Council, a governing body comprising a

📺 **THE THREE DOCTORS**
by Bob Baker
& Dave Martin
starring Jon Pertwee,
Patrick Troughton
and William Hartnell
as the Doctor
First broadcast:
30/12/1972–20/01/1973

Chancellor and Cardinals, with each Cardinal in turn the head of the various Chapters of the Time Lords, such as the Arcalians, the Patrexes and the Prydonians. In later periods, the High Council was expanded to include the Castellan (the head of the Chancellery Guard). While the

President was selected by ballot, a retiring President could name his successor, who would usually be elected unopposed.

Rassilon's influence was not merely political, however, and he continued to be a scientific pioneer. He altered the Time Lords' genetic make-up, giving them the Rassilon Imprimatur – symbiotic nuclei which made them time-sensitive and allowed them to undergo time travel in safety, and which may also have facilitated their other great power: complete bodily renewal, or regeneration. An Amplified Panatropic Net was developed: an electronic repository for the mind of every Time Lord, harvested at the moment of death. This incorporated – or perhaps simply became known as – the Matrix, which used the accumulated knowledge of the Time Lords to predict future events and guide their actions

THE DEADLY ASSASSIN
by Robert Holmes
starring Tom Baker
as the Doctor
First broadcast:
30/10/1976–20/11/1976

A BEGINNER'S GUIDE TO TRANSDIMENSIONAL ENGINEERING

EQUIPMENT: ➤ One small box (A) ➤ One large box (B) ➤ One subject (L) with two eyes and an open mind

STEP 1
Position **L** at point **x**.

STEP 2
Place **A** next to **B** at point **y**, at a distance of 1 metre from **L** at point **x**.

STEP 3
Make comparative evaluation of relative sizes of **A** and **B**, i.e. ask **L** which box looks larger.

STEP 4
Keep **L** at point **x**; keep **A** at point **y**; move **B** to point **z**, at a distance of approx 1 metre from point **x**.

STEP 5
Make comparative evaluation of relative sizes of **A** and **B**, i.e. ask **L** which box looks larger.

STEP 6
Without moving **B** from point **z**, place **B** inside **A** at point **y**. (**L** may now move from point **x**.)

NOTE: Many species have found Step 6 difficult to complete, and some have dismissed it as 'silly'. For the Time Lords, however, it was a key discovery.

in the present. Rassilon also developed theories and practices of temporal fission and invented new defences for the planet, with a quantum force field repelling any assault from space and the Transduction Barriers preventing the unauthorised approach of a time machine. Dematerialisation technology was refined too, first through experimentation with tachyonics and then in warp-matrix engineering. This technology was applied not just in time-travel capsules but also in weaponry: the Demat Gun could remove all traces of its victim from all of space and time. It was so powerful that even its theoretical existence was eventually hidden from the Time Lords.

THE INVASION OF TIME
by David Agnew
starring Tom Baker
as the Doctor
First broadcast:
04/02/1978–11/03/1978

With such scientific dominance came tremendous responsibility and, in their earliest epochs at least, they seem to have used and abused their powers in equal measure as they began to encounter other powerful races. On the one hand, they became a great force for good, time-looping the planet of the voracious Fendahl, ridding the cosmos of the Great Vampires – which they fought and destroyed using mighty bowships – and leading the Fledgling Empires to triumph against the omnivorous Racnoss. Although single representatives of both the Vampires and the Racnoss actually escaped, the Gallifreyans' aims were genocidal. Their other early interventions were often notable for their cruelty and arrogance. The Time Lords' involvement on Minyos was catastrophic: welcomed as gods, they gave the Minyans technology that would ultimately destroy the planet.

These events, and the Minyan Intervention in particular, gave rise to the official Time Lord policies of non-violence and non-interference in the affairs of other races. Alongside the Constitution and its Five Great Principles were the Laws of Time and The Worshipful and Ancient Law of Gallifrey, again seemingly drawn up by Rassilon. In a nutshell, these forbade any Time Lord from crossing his own time stream, from meeting his different selves, or from altering history in any way, and outlawed capital punishment and genocide, with a prison planet called Shada established as an alternative. The Time Lords accepted some responsibility for the protection of lesser species, but rarely allowed this to compromise their policy of non-interference. Once characterised by the Doctor as galactic ticket inspectors, their involvement in universal affairs was largely limited to policing unlicensed time travel – a self-interested policy that ensured they maintained their own position of dominance.

THE DALEKS AND TIME TRAVEL

Though the Time Lords were renowned for jealously guarding their secrets, they are not the only race to have developed time travel. There are – or have been – several naturally time-sensitive species, including the Tharils and the Reapers, and even some beings, like the Chronovores, the Eternals, the Guardians, the Trickster and the Weeping Angels, that seem to exist outside time itself. A few other species have invented or simply purloined time-travel technology, notably the Sontarans, the Cybermen, the Graske, the Family of Blood and even the human race. But perhaps the most interesting are the Daleks, who seem to have discovered the principles of time travel from the Time Lords – maybe even directly from the Doctor.

Their earliest attempts involved unstable time-corridor technology (which may have evolved from warp-matrix engineering). This enabled them to establish crude bridgeheads into the past, such as from a Dalek-controlled 22nd-century Earth back to the 1970s. A second saw them using similar methods to reach from Skaro to England in 1866 and 1966. A third was part of a Dalek attempt to take over Gallifrey by ensnaring the Doctor in a time corridor stretching back to 1980s London.

It is clear from these attempts that the Daleks were aware of the threat posed by both the Doctor and the Time Lords, and a team of Dalek scientists eventually built a prototype Dalek time machine in an attempt to hunt down his first incarnation. This ship was an advance on their earlier attempts: although based on inferior technology, it was also dimensionally transcendental, easier to steer and appeared to be as fast as the Doctor's craft. A second Dalek time machine was used in an attempt to track the Doctor down after he'd fled to Ancient Egypt with a Taranium Core. The Doctor was dismissive of these machines. They were, in his view, extremely dangerous in construction, possibly because they had no stable link to an equivalent of the Eye of Harmony.

The Seventh Doctor had a seemingly final encounter with a time-capable Dalek Empire. These Daleks were able to move as fluidly through time as through space, and had travelled from Skaro's far future to London in 1963 looking for the Hand Of Omega, perhaps hoping to take their time technology to the next level by opening their own Eye of Harmony. These Daleks moved a giant battleship through time, and appeared to exist simultaneously both in the 1960s and in the far future. At this point, the Doctor destroyed Skaro, perhaps realising that the Daleks were getting just too good at time travel...

Future historians may argue that this was the action that provoked Dalek retaliation on a massive scale, changing the Time War from a cold war of isolated incidents to all-out Armageddon. With both sides using their time-equipped battle fleets to wreak havoc throughout history, their conflict was so fearsome and devastating that only the tiniest details have escaped the Timelock put in place at the culmination of the War.

REMEMBRANCE OF THE DALEKS
by Ben Aaronovitch
starring Sylvester McCoy as the Doctor
First broadcast:
05/10/1988–26/10/1988

From this point, the majority of Time Lord society began to ossify as they retreated behind their Transduction Barriers to simply observe and record the universe, while abandoning what they now thought of as 'the barren road' of technology – they were content to use their vast

accomplishments but lost any true notion of their significance or even of how they worked. Over the course of some ten million years, the scientific background behind their artefacts and ceremonies was gradually lost in myth and legend, and pomp and circumstance replaced wisdom and insight.

There were, though, sections of the Time Lord hierarchy that refused to accept the new precepts, maintaining clandestine operations and flouting the official Laws. Political expediency would sometimes prevail, with tribunals being set up on various occasions

with the power to sit in judgment on criminals and give sentences that might, after all, involve a death penalty – among those disintegrated from time and space in such a manner was the War Lord, leader of a race that had captured and manipulated thousands of human beings, most of whom had died fighting their war games. Before his death, the War Lord had faced a Time Lord tribunal – there would be many of these over the next few centuries, though whether their status was official is not known. It is even possible that these tribunals were in fact among the activities of the mysterious Celestial Intervention Agency...

The CIA was a top-secret organisation of Time Lords with no qualms about maintaining an interest in outside affairs. They used agents, willing or otherwise, to manipulate events beyond Gallifrey, often acting for the best reasons, but sometimes from darker motives. Much evidence is lost in the mists of time, but the CIA may have had a hand in events on planets as far apart as Peladon, Solos, Spiridon and Karn, and – most disastrously for the Time Lords – Skaro. An agent known as the Doctor was despatched to Skaro; his mission to avert the genesis of the Daleks. This would later be seen as the first shot in what became known as the Last Great Time War, a cataclysmic conflict that eventually brought about the near-total extinction of both Daleks and Time Lords and the destruction of their home worlds.

GENESIS OF THE DALEKS
by **Terry Nation**
starring Tom Baker
as the Doctor
First broadcast:
08/03/1975–12/04/1975

The details of the Time War are more obscure than anything else in the Time Lords' murky history, though the battle with the Daleks seems to have corrupted the last traces of the Gallifreyans' once-elevated morality. The attrition of war changed the Time Lords, right to the core, and they fulfilled their dangerous potential. What is known is that few seemed to have survived, on either side – only the Doctor walked away from the final battle, though he later discovered that there had been a few other escapees from the devastation,

including the Dalek Emperor, the Cult of Skaro and the Master. It subsequently transpired that both sides had attempted to dodge the annihilation on a massive scale. The Cult of Skaro had concealed millions of Daleks in a Time Lord prison ship hidden in the Void. And, aware of the impending destruction of their world, the Time Lords implanted a psychic link between Gallifrey and the mind of the Master.

The link's point of physical contact was a diamond, a Whitepoint Star, which the resurrected Rassilon sent to the planet Earth. The Master – driven insane by the centuries-long incessant drumbeat of the psychic link in his mind – retrieved the diamond and used it to establish contact with Gallifrey in its timelocked final moments. The entire world of Gallifrey was able to follow the link to Earth. Gallifrey would actually replace the planet Earth in space, before the Time Lords initiated their Final Sanction: the rupturing of the Time Vortex, destroying all of creation apart from the Time Lord race, who would continue as disembodied consciousnesses, finally freed from the constraints of time itself.

THE END OF TIME
by Russell T Davies
starring David Tennant as the Doctor
First broadcast:
25/12/2009–01/01/2010

The Doctor realised that the breaking of the Timelock had allowed the return to this universe not only of every threat from the Time War – the Skaro Degradations, the Horde of Travesties, the Nightmare Child, the Couldhavebeen King with his Army of Meanwhiles and Never-weres, and, of course, the Daleks themselves – but also of his own deadly and amoral race. He broke the link to the Whitepoint Star and sent Gallifrey and the Time Lords back into the hell of the final moments of the Time War. The Doctor was, once again, the Last of the Time Lords.

Time-Travel Capsules

With the science of time travel understood and perfected and its power source secured, the Time Lords developed a range of travel capsules. They used transdimensional engineering to map an external shell onto a potentially infinite internal dimension, allowing the creation of a 'living' machine, a transportation device that was grown and nurtured in the Gallifreyan Black Hole Shipyards rather than simply built, and which was able to develop a symbiotic relationship with any or all of its operating crew of up to six Time Lords. Over countless millennia, Time Lord scientists continued to refine, update and upgrade these capsules, with several different 'Marks' of a hundred or more 'Types', for example the Type 40 Mark III.

A MADMAN WITH A BOX

The TARDIS has been ravaged by the force of the regeneration energy bursting out of the Doctor as he changes into his eleventh form. The external windows have blown out, and the console is in flames, with buttresses crashing to the floor and debris pouring down, while the new Doctor struggles to regain control over his ship.

The TARDIS plunges towards planet Earth, crash-landing in the back garden of a house in the English village of Leadworth. There he meets young Amelia Pond and starts to deal with a scary crack in her bedroom wall. But the TARDIS engines are phasing and the Doctor needs to stabilise them with a five-minute hop into the future. Instead, the TARDIS brings him back to Leadworth twelve years later.

While the Doctor deals with a dangerous multiform and its would-be jailers, the TARDIS regenerates itself, inside and out...

JOURNEY LOG
The Eleventh Hour

There is a split in the skin of the world, which has brought together two parts of space and time that should never have touched. On one side is Amelia Pond's bedroom in Leadworth; on the other is an Atraxi prison cell, whose occupant – Prisoner Zero – has escaped through the crack. When the Doctor

📺 **THE ELEVENTH HOUR**
by Steven Moffat
Starring Matt Smith as the Doctor
First broadcast: 03/04/2010

EXT. AMELIA'S GARDEN – 1996 NIGHT

The TARDIS lies there in the smashed remains of the garden shed. It's charred and smoking (PRAC FX), like it got a bit burned on re-entry.

Little AMELIA is approaching nervously through the garden, clutching her torch. She shines the torch on the big blue box – the base of which is facing her. She reaches out, touches it. Ow! Hot!

She stares at the huge blue box, wonderingly, and – WHAM!!

The police box doors fly open, up the way, falling outward like the flaps in the top of a jack-in-the-box. Light and smoke stream up from within (PRAC FX).

Amelia: falters back a few steps. What is this, what's happening. Frightened, but doesn't run, keeps watching.

A rope flies up from inside the box, something heavy attached at the end. It thuds into grass at Amelia's feet – she startles back. A grappling hook!

The rope tightens, the grappling hook is dragged back, catches on the TARDIS base, anchors there. The rope and hook strain and shift, taking the weight of something. Someone is climbing up!

Grunts and scuffles from within. Then a hand gripping on to the edge of the base, then another hand, and then, a face! THE DOCTOR.

His hair is soaking wet, his eyes are wild and dancing. And he's looking right at Amelia. Amelia stares back at him. A silence.

>   THE DOCTOR
> Can I have an apple?

THE ELEVENTH HOUR
by Steven Moffat

attempts to close the breach, he inadvertently attracts the attention of the Atraxi forces seeking the escaped Prisoner Zero, placing the entire planet Earth under threat of incineration. The newly regenerated Time Lord has just twenty minutes to save the world from an Atraxi fission blast.

Amy Pond

Working as a kissogram by the time the TARDIS returns in 2008, Amy Pond has grown up obsessed by 'the raggedy Doctor' she met as a child. She has seen four psychiatrists, who have all insisted that the Doctor was a figment of her imagination (she bit them), and just about everybody in Leadworth knows of her fixation. As a child, she drew pictures and made glove puppets of him, and later made her boyfriend Rory dress up as him.

Prisoner Zero

An inter-dimensional multiform, with a lifespan measured in millennia and the ability to assume any appearance via a psychic link with a living but dormant mind. Having escaped its Atraxi cell, Prisoner Zero takes on the forms of coma victims in Leadworth Hospital, incorporating their dreams into its physical manifestation – a man with a dog, or a mother with her children. It is recaptured when it takes Amy's form and the Doctor encourages her to dream of the alien in its original shape. The multiform reverts to its natural face-tendril state.

Rory Williams

Rory is Amy Pond's boyfriend, and has known her for most of their lives. He suspects that she's only with him because he bears a passing resemblance to the Doctor, and her obsession with the stranger from her childhood prompted Rory to train in medicine. He didn't do well enough to become a doctor, and ended up as a nurse at Leadworth Hospital. He is the first person in Leadworth to notice that coma victims appear to be wandering the streets. In the two years following the Atraxi capture of their prisoner, Rory and Amy get engaged.

THE CHAMELEON CIRCUIT

Only the exterior of a TARDIS exists as a real space-time event. This outer-plasmic shell is mapped onto one of the interior continua. In other words, a pair of doors leads into and out of the active control room.

The exterior shell is driven by the Chameleon Circuit, controlled by the capsule's operator via a pop-up panel on the main console. In the Type 40 TARDIS Mark I, the operator can input instructions in machine code, with a graphic of the capsule exterior displayed on the main scanner screen. When a precise mathematical model of a real 'event' (e.g. a pyramid) is input, the external shell converts to replicate the appearance of that event.

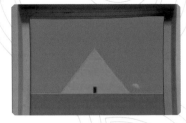

📺 **ATTACK OF THE CYBERMEN**
by Paula Moore
Starring Colin Baker as the Doctor
First broadcast: 05/01/1986–12/01/1986

In a fully operational TARDIS, the Chameleon Circuit usually operates automatically. When the capsule materialises, the location is scanned and the Circuit selects an appropriate disguise that will allow the capsule to blend in with its surroundings – after departing Gallifrey, the Doctor's borrowed TARDIS took various forms, including an ionic column and a sedan chair, before converting to a police box on arrival in 1960s London. On the TARDIS's next trip, however – an unplanned journey some 100,000 years into Earth's prehistory – the Circuit malfunctioned, and the exterior shell became stuck in its police box form.

The Doctor has occasionally attempted to fix the faulty Circuit. At the end of his fourth incarnation, he enlisted the help of the people of the planet Logopolis in using Block Transfer Computation to overlay a precise mathematical model of an authentic Earth police box on the TARDIS to rectify the defect. On that occasion, interference from the Master disrupted the Logopolitans' calculations and caused the TARDIS to shrink with the Doctor inside.

The Sixth Doctor later effected a partial repair, restoring the TARDIS's ability to disguise itself. He had limited success, and the time machine materialised as a cabinet, a pipe organ and a gateway before reverting to its familiar form. The Doctor quickly realised that he was more than happy with the TARDIS in its police box shape, although Donna Noble – in the wake of a biological metacrisis – once began to advise the Tenth Doctor on how to effect a permanent repair:

INT. TARDIS – NIGHT

                    DONNA
    Brilliant! Fantastic! Molto
    bene! Great big universe,
    packed into my brain! D'you
    know, you could fix that
    chameleon circuit if you just
    tried hotbinding the fragment-
    links and superseding the
    binary, binary
              (can't stop)
    Binary, binary, binary, binary,
    binary, binary – I'm fine!

JOURNEY'S END
by Russell T Davies

Blending in

The default appearance of an
undisguised TARDIS is a grey
metal cabinet with a sliding door.

The Doctor's TARDIS is unique
in remaining in one exterior
form more or less constantly.
The TARDISes used by other
renegade Time Lords have
taken many shapes and sizes:

>> Beach hut >> Bi-plane >> Block of brown stone >> Block of ice
>> Box >> Cabinet >> Computer bank >> Concorde
>> Corinthian column >> Cupboard >> Fireplace >> Grandfather clock
>> Horsebox >> Igloo >> Ionic column >> Iron maiden
>> Melkur, a calcified statue >> Motorbike >> Obelisk
>> Copies of the Doctor's police box >> Potted shrub
>> Reflective pyramid >> Rock >> Rocket >> Saxon sarcophagus
>> Sepulchre >> Spaceship >> Stagecoach
>> Statue of Queen Victoria >> Tree

THE POLICE BOX

A brief history

By the early 1960s, police boxes were unremarkable sights on Britain's streets and in police dramas like *Dixon of Dock Green* and *Z Cars* on British television. A call box or post from which the local police and fire departments could be contacted by police officers and the public had actually been an American innovation soon after the invention of the telephone in 1876; several US cities including New York, Detroit and Chicago installed variations on a call-box theme during the 1870s and 1880s, and the idea crossed the Atlantic to Glasgow in 1880.

The classic police box design was pioneered in Newcastle in 1929, and over the next decade what became known as the Metropolitan Police Box designed by Gilbert Mackenzie-Trench was introduced throughout London: a dark blue kiosk, made at first of wood and then concrete, with an electric lamp on the roof. The lamp was flashed to attract the attention of nearby police officers on the beat, and each box contained a telephone with a direct line to the local police station. Behind the double doors was, typically, a stool and table, a fire extinguisher and a small electric fire – officers could shelter in the police box if the weather was inclement, and many would sit inside to eat their sandwiches. Police officers could also temporarily hold apprehended criminals inside the kiosk. The public were permitted to access a hand-held telephone in a cabinet at the front of the box in order to contact the police if they witnessed a crime or an accident. The boxes gradually became a crucial part of police communications.

In the mid 1960s, however, personal radios were developed and became standard issue for all police officers. The police box quickly became redundant, and the boxes had been mostly decommissioned and removed from the streets by the early 1970s. By the end of the twentieth century, this once commonplace sight could be spotted in just a handful of locations in the British Isles, but was now better known – worldwide – as the iconic outward appearance of a famous time machine...

Why a police box?

A small team at the BBC discussed and developed ideas for a Saturday teatime serial throughout 1962 and 1963. As they firmed up their ideas for 'Dr. Who', the concept of a time-travelling capsule was quick to surface as the means by which the series' heroes could venture through periods in history and to other worlds. By early May 1963, in an early briefing document written by C.E. Webber, the notion of the ship disguising itself as 'something humdrum' was already being discussed:

DR. WHO'S "MACHINE"

When we consider what this looks like, we are in danger of either Science Fiction or Fairytale labelling. If it is a transparent plastic bubble we are with all the lowgrade spacefiction of cartoon strip and soap-opera. If we scotch this by positing something humdrum, say, passing through some common object in street such as a night-watchman's shelter to arrive inside a marvellous contrivance of quivering electronics, then we simply have a version of the dear old Magic Door.

Therefore, we do not see the machine at all; or rather it is visible only as an absence of visability, a shape of nothingness (Inlaid, into surrounding picture). Dr. Who has achieved this "disappearance" by covering the outside with light-resistant paint (a recognised research project today). Thus our characters can bump into it, run their hands over its shape, partly disappear by partly entering it, and disappear entirely when the door closes behind them. It can be put into an apparently empty van. Wherever they go some contemprary disguise has to be found for it. Many visual possibilities can be worked out. The discovery of the old man and investigation of his machine would occupy most of the first episode, which would be called:-

"NOTHING AT THE END OF THE LANE"

The machine is unreliable, being faulty. A recurrent problem is to find spares. How to get thin gauge platinum wire in B.C.1566? Moreover, Dr. Who has lost his memory, so they have to learn to use it, by a process of trial and error, keeping records of knobs pressed and results (This is the fuel for many a long story). After several near-calamities they institute a safeguard: one of their number is left in the machine when the others go outside, so that at the end of an agreed time, they can be fetched back into their own era. This provides a suspense element in any given danger: can they survive till the moment of recall? Attack on recaller etc.

Original 1963 background notes

BBC Head of Drama Sydney Newman rejected this idea of an invisible ship as 'Not visual ... What do we see?' A 'tangible symbol' was needed, he said. A revised briefing document on 15 May 1963 recorded that 'a police box standing in the street' had been settled on, 'but anyone entering it is immediately inside an extensive electronic contrivance'. The police box was the idea of BBC staff writer Anthony Coburn, who subsequently went freelance and scripted *Doctor Who*'s very first story. Coburn apparently suggested the police box disguise after noticing one on a street corner near his office.

THE TARDIS POLICE BOX 1963–2010

1963–1976

1976–1980

The original TARDIS exterior, designed by Peter Brachacki

➤➤ There is a St John Ambulance logo on the right-hand door ➤➤ The lock is in the left-hand door, though it temporarily moved to the right-hand door in 1968 ➤➤ The sign on the telephone cabinet moved from the left- to the right-hand door for several stories in 1966–1967; it moved back to the left in 1968, and was replaced around the same time, with a new background colour and different lettering, changed from white on blue to white on black in 1971 ➤➤ The roof was reduced in height in 1966 ➤➤ The entire box was repainted in 1971.

The second TARDIS exterior, designed by Barry Newbery

➤➤ The phone cabinet sign changed back to white text on a blue background with a similar layout to the original, but the word 'officers' lost its 's' ➤➤ This fresh design dropped several features of the Metropolitan Police Box, most notably swapping the stacked roof for a new, flat version

➤➤ A different rooftop lamp was used for one story in 1979 – actually a rotating lamp from a police car.

1980–1989

The fibreglass exterior, designed by Tom Yardley-Jones

➤➤ The stacked roof was reinstated to create a more authentic prop

➤➤ The front and rear panels could be switched to allow the door to be opened from the left or the right as needed

➤➤ The newly detachable phone cabinet plaque varied during this period, sometimes restoring the original wording but sometimes featuring the revised phrase 'officer and cars respond to all calls'.

1996

The TV movie version, designed by Richard Hudolin

➤➤ Designed with reference to the 1963 and 1980 versions, this was constructed from wood with a very weather-beaten look to the paint finish

➤➤ The Police Public Call Box signs near the top of the box were backlit, while a completely new lamp was constructed for the roof ➤➤ A Yale-type lock on the door moved aside to reveal a key-hole for the ankh-shaped key.

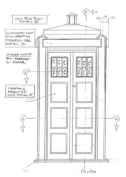

2005–2010

POLICE TELEPHONE
FREE
FOR USE OF
PUBLIC
ADVICE & ASSISTANCE
OBTAINABLE IMMEDIATELY
OFFICER & CARS
RESPOND TO ALL CALLS
PULL TO OPEN

The resurrection, designed by Edward Thomas

》 Edward Thomas and designer Colin Richmond decided decided on a larger, more solid-looking police box – wider, taller, and with bigger doors **》** The traditional Yale lock was updated to the new Era make **》** The windows were enlarged and were given an interior illumination to suggest the immense power of the machine within **》** There were two models of each of two slightly different versions, with a fifth later made in fibreglass **》** The phone cabinet sign now used black lettering on a metallic background and repeated the 1980s wording.

POLICE TELEPHONE
FREE
FOR USE OF
PUBLIC
ADVICE & ASSISTANCE
OBTAINABLE IMMEDIATELY
OFFICERS & CARS
RESPOND TO ALL CALLS
PULL TO OPEN

The current model, designed by Edward Thomas
▶▶ It has the same dimensions as its immediate predecessor, but with white-framed windows ▶▶ It has a new finish in a brighter blue ▶▶ There is a new rooftop lamp taken from a ship ▶▶ The St John Ambulance sticker

has now made a return ▶▶ The original wording ('officers and cars') of the phone cabinet sign has been restored ▶▶ Showrunner Steven Moffat wanted the prop to closely resemble the one used in the 1960s movies starring Peter Cushing.

First Impressions

'It's a police box! What on earth's it doing here? These things are usually on the street...'

'We can travel anywhere in that old box, as you call it. Regardless of space and time.'

'I'm sure there's something strange about that police box. Look he's got a key for it... He's going inside!'

'A police box? I don't believe it!'

'It's a 20th-century police box, isn't it? How did a thing like that get inside my museum?'

'Camouflage, General. It's not really a police box. It's a spaceship.'

'Are you trying to tell me you can absorb the total output of this complex in a police box?'

'What do you plan to do in there?'
'Make myself a cup of coffee.'

'There are no Type 40s in service.
They're out of commission. Obsolete.'

'Come along now, Doctor... police boxes don't go careering around all over the place.'

'What exactly is that contraption?'
'It's his personal transport. Look – "Police"...'

'It seems to be stuck in this ridiculous shape.
I wonder what it was imitating...?'

'And since it has no call to be here, the art
lies in the fact that it is here.'

'That's funny. That's very
peculiar indeed...'

'There's got to be a trick to this.'

'What is this?' 'It may be the only glimpse you ever get of my TARDIS.'

'But there won't be any room.'
'You are in for a surprise!'

'This mysterious most is.'

'It's called the TARDIS.'
'Really? Couldn't we take it for a bit of a spin?'

'Maximum alert. If the Doctor is involved, look out for a police telephone box.'

'Its cloaking device got stuck on a previous misadventure. I like it like this.'

'Naah, tell you what, let's go in here.'
'You can't just hide in a wooden box –!'

'That old woman's staring.'
'Probably wondering what four people
can do inside a small wooden box.'

'So what happens inside that thing then?'
'D'you wanna see?' 'No, I don't think so.'

'Come back to the TARDIS.'
'No way. That box is too... weird.'

'Your spaceship's made of wood. There's not much room. We'd be a bit intimate.'

'Oh! And this is it! If I might, Doctor...?
One last adventure...?'

'Little blue box! Just like you said!
Right then – off we go! Come on, Doctor,
show me the stars!'

Pull to open

The exterior shell of the TARDIS is theoretically impregnable. Its external doors contain a sophisticated locking mechanism: a double-curtain trimonic barrier requiring a cipher-indent key. This has usually looked like an ordinary Yale key, although the Third Doctor began using an ankh-shaped device that was also used by the Fourth and Eighth Doctors. The lock itself is found in the right-hand police box door.

Other than the Doctor, his granddaughter Susan kept her own key, and the Fourth and Fifth Doctors occasionally gave spare keys to trusted companions like Sarah Jane Smith, Romana and Tegan. More recently, Rose Tyler, Captain Jack Harkness, Martha Jones and Donna Noble have all been given their own keys. While earlier incarnations would sometimes conceal a key in their shoes, the Seventh Doctor kept a spare in a secret compartment above the letter 'P' in the Police Public Call Box sign at the top of the external doors. The key has some remote connection to the TARDIS itself; when the time machine is nearby, the key glows and becomes hot.

When the First Doctor and Susan left Gallifrey, there was a complex locking mechanism: placing the key in one of twenty wrong positions would cause the entire lock to melt; only the Doctor or Susan knew the twenty-first, correct position that would open the door. Perhaps because he was joined by other travelling companions, the Doctor soon modified the lock, briefly replacing it with a removable version. By the end of his second incarnation, the Doctor had installed a metabolism detector in the lock to prevent unauthorised access. Towards the end of his life, the Seventh Doctor concealed the true exterior lock behind a standard Yale keyhole.

The most recent mechanism used by the Ninth, Tenth and Eleventh Doctors resembles a twenty-first-century Era make lock and key. But the Tenth Doctor discovered that he and his TARDIS were now so closely connected that he could open the door with a click of his fingers – an ability the Eleventh Doctor has retained.

EXT. AMY'S GARDEN - 2010 NIGHT

The Doctor raises a hand, and snaps his fingers –
– and the police box doors crack slightly open. Blazing light streams from inside.

On Amy, the light spilling over her face, a girl in a dream. She steps slowly forward.

THE ELEVENTH HOUR
by Steven Moffat

THE REAL-WORLD INTERFACE

During *Doctor Who*'s original run from 1963, it was usual either to avoid a direct view of the ship's interior or to show a black void-like space. Since the first episode of the 2005 series, the view through the open police box doors has been of the vast space inside the TARDIS. This has sometimes been achieved by adding a computer-generated image to the picture during the final editing. But it has more often been accomplished during filming through the use of a photographic backdrop precisely positioned inside the police box prop. Special care has to be taken by directors to ensure that camera angles give viewers the correct perspective on the background interior image.

```
EXT. AMELIA'S GARDEN - 2008 DAY

The TARDIS! Not battered and charred any more -
magnificent and blue, with glowing, golden windows.

THE DOCTOR is skidding to a halt in front of it.
His face: as giddy and thrilled as a child. Grinning.

He puts the key in the lock.

                    THE DOCTOR
             Okay then! What have you
             got for me this time?

And in he goes.


INT. TARDIS - 2008 DAY

We keep tight on police box
doors, as THE DOCTOR pushes
through them. Then tight on his
face as he stares, delighted at
his new TARDIS.

                    THE DOCTOR
        Look at you! Oh, you sexy thing!

He goes past us into the TARDIS - we hold on the police
box doors, just seeing his shadow, as he stands, arms
outspread, celebrating his new domain.

                    THE DOCTOR (CONT'D)
        Look at you!!
```

THE ELEVENTH HOUR
by Steven Moffat

2

THERE'S A WHOLE WORLD IN HERE

Fourteen years after her first sight of the TARDIS, Amy Pond is finally invited inside. She is confronted with an impossibly vast space. There are huge curving coppery walls and floors, at least three different levels, stairs and walkways... And, at its heart, stands a six-panelled console covered in controls, buttons, levers, a typewriter, a monitor screen, a computer keyboard, a telephone, compasses and sextants, countless devices, some alien, some familiar. A large column of wood-framed glass links the console to an enormous circular device at the apex of the domed ceiling. Inside the column are peculiar glass objects that rise and fall with the rhythm of a heartbeat.

There's little time for her to take it all in, though. Scarcely pausing for breath, the Doctor whisks them off to the end of the 33rd century. The monitor screen on the console shows the view outside the ship – Starship UK...

THE BEAST BELOW
by Steven Moffat
Starring Matt Smith
as the Doctor
First broadcast:
10/4/2010

JOURNEY LOG:
The Beast Below

The Doctor and Amy uncover the workings of a police state. Everything is falling into disrepair. The Winders wind up the powerless equipment to keep everything functioning. People are going missing. There are tales of a beast in the depths of the spaceship. Yet nobody is talking about any of it. Nobody protests. The British people have voted to forget.

Solar flares

In the 29th century, Earth scientists realised that solar flares were about to devastate the planet, making its biosphere uninhabitable for at least 5,000 years. The human race fled its home world. Some set out to found

distant colonies such as Galsec. One self-selecting elite chose cryogenic suspension aboard the enormous space station *Nerva*. One way or another, everybody left the planet. But the people of Britain remained, without the funds or resources they needed to escape.

```
INT. TARDIS - DAY

THE DOCTOR and AMY are watching the
street scene on the wall-mounted
monitor.

                    AMY
        But you said it was a
        spaceship.

                THE DOCTOR
        It is.

The Doctor touches a control.

FX: On the screen we start cutting
round various views of the spaceship.
```

THE BEAST BELOW
by Steven Moffat

Star Whales

A species that once lived in deep space, first encountered by Earth's spacefaring pioneers, the Star Whales would guide these early space travellers through cosmic hazards. As the solar flares began

to strike planet Earth, the last surviving Star Whale heard the screams of Britain's children and came to help. But when it reached Earth, the desperate British government trapped it, building a massive spacecraft around it, and using it to power the flight of the entire population.

Starship UK

The spaceship comprises many linked tower blocks of steel, each containing the populace of entire cities and counties. But Britain didn't evacuate just the population – they took some of the buildings, too. Buckingham Palace and the Tower of London are among the tourist attractions preserved on board. All this, yet the engines don't work. It is a fake spaceship. The whole unwieldy structure floats through the stars with the Star Whale at its heart. The beast has been wired into Starship UK, constantly tortured just to keep it moving through the stars.

Smilers

Throughout Starship UK are the mechanical
Smilers, watching everyone, teaching the
children, enforcing the law. They sit in glass
and metal booths protruding from the walls
of the spaceship. They are named for the fixed
smiles on their plastic faces, but their heads
can revolve to display a frown of disapproval
or a demonic fanged snarl. They oversee the
disappearances of under-achieving children
– who become slaves among the ship's inner
workings – and lawbreaking adults, who are
fed to the Star Whale.

BUT IT WAS JUST A TELEPHONE BOX!

Amy Pond is the latest in a long line of bewildered people to have stepped through the doors of the Doctor's blue box and into an inexplicable and magical world. The first, way back when the Doctor had not long fled Gallifrey with his granddaughter, were Ian Chesterton and Barbara Wright. Schoolteachers who had followed their pupil home, hoping to talk to the girl's grandfather about her erratic schoolwork, Ian and Barbara found only a police box in a junkyard. There they confronted a defensive old man, who tried to brush off their questions but was unable to prevent them forcing their way into the box.

AN UNEARTHLY CHILD
by Anthony Coburn
Starring William Hartnell as the Doctor
First broadcast:
23/11/1963–14/12/1963

Inside was a gleaming room, many times larger than the box that contained it, its white walls covered in circular indentations, with a small television-like screen mounted in one corner. There were assorted items from different time periods scattered around – an antique clock, a statue, a chair. But the room was dominated by a six-sided console covered in instruments and gauges, levers and switches. A cylindrical glass column containing further mysterious instruments emerged

from the centre of this console, and began a rhythmic rise and fall when the Doctor, minutes later, set the machine itself in motion.

Refusing to release the teachers, the Doctor explained that Ian and Barbara were inside a machine that travelled in space and time, using technology far beyond human understanding. Far beyond the Doctor's

understanding, too, as it turned out – not only was it faulty; he couldn't control it either. The four travellers were off on an adventure in space and time, and none of them knew when or where they'd turn up next...

'I walked all round it!'

'Well, it's huge! And... well... the outside is just... well...'

'If this isn't a police box, what is it?' 'Well... this machine is for travelling through time and relative dimensions in space.' 'Come again?'

'That is the dematerialising control and that, over yonder, is the horizontal hold. Up there is the scanner, those are the doors, that is a chair with a panda on it – sheer poetry, dear boy!'

'I can't believe it. It's so big! Where are we?' 'Oh it's the TARDIS. It's my home, or at least it has been for a considerable number of years.'

'The TARDIS is dimensionally transcendental.' 'What does that mean?' 'It means that it's bigger inside than out.'

'Aren't you going to say that it's bigger on the inside than it is on the outside? Everybody else does.' 'That's pretty obvious.'

'So this is what you've been doing with UNIT funds and equipment all this time. How's it done? Some sort of optical illusion?'

'To the rational mind, nothing is inexplicable. Only unexplained.' 'So... Explain to me how this... TARDIS is larger on the inside than the out.'

'I saw a blue box!' 'Quite right, we're inside it. It's called the TARDIS. How's your transcendental dimensionalism?'

'But why is it so much bigger inside than it is outside?' 'Oh, the Doctor told me that was because it was dimensionally transcendental.'

'Well, there must be intelligent life at the end of this lot. ... Hullo? Anybody receiving me? ... I'd like to speak to the pilot.'

'I must say, all this is going to be rather difficult to explain in my report.'

'It's not possible...'

'Good heavens... It's amazing. It isn't of this planet.'

'Look, I'm finding all this a bit disturbing. Cybermen, now Daleks... Time travel... in an organ!' 'You'll get used to it.'

'D'you know, it's actually bigger inside –' 'I know.' '– than it is on the outside.' 'I know, I know!'

'Here, how d'you do that?' 'It's bigger on the inside than it is on the outside.' 'Don't come all clever dick with me. What's going on?'

'Low-tech? Grace, this is a Type 40 TARDIS, able to take you to any planet in the universe and to any date in that planet's existence.'

'Where do you want to start?' 'Um... the inside's bigger than the outside?' 'Yes.' 'It's alien.' 'Yup.'

'Welcome to the TARDIS.' 'Much bigger on the inside.' 'You'd better be.'

'This place is impossible! It's superb! How do you get the outside around the inside?' 'Like I'd give you the secret, yeah.' 'I almost feel better about being defeated. We never stood a chance.'

'Exterminate!'

'I demand you tell me right now -- where am I?' 'Inside the TARDIS.' 'The what?' 'The TARDIS.' 'That's not even a proper word.'

'How does it do that? It's wood! It's like a box with that room just.... crammed in. It's bigger on the inside!' 'Is it? I hadn't noticed.'

'No. Way.' 'What do you think?' 'Can I have a coffee?'

'This is nonsense!' 'That's one word for it!' 'Complete and utter, wonderful nonsense. How very, very silly!'

'Ah. Right. Yes. Bigger on the inside. D'you like it?' 'I thought it'd be cleaner.' 'Cleaner?! I could take you back home, right now!'

'Well? Anything you want to say? Any passing remarks. I've heard them all.' 'I'm in my nightie.'

ORIGINS

The story of *Doctor Who* is unique in many ways, not least in that the series evolved from no single creative vision. Sydney Newman, the BBC's Head of Drama in 1963, was the main impetus behind the new show, appointing its first producer – Verity Lambert – and almost certainly suggesting its name, but the end result was the fruit of months of input from several different people. Many long-lasting aspects of the series were dreamed up or hinted at by one or more of the figures who were there at the very beginning, notably the nature and appearance of the TARDIS itself.

Donald Wilson, the BBC's Head of Serials was the first to propose that the new teatime science-fiction series might feature a machine 'not only for going forward and backwards in time, but into space, and into all kinds of matter (e.g. a drop of oil, a molecule, under the ocean, etc.)'. This notion drove the initial ideas for *Doctor Who*'s first story, which was to see the time travellers landing back in the real world but reduced to microscopic size. The debut serial actually presented an entirely different adventure, but the original concept was revived for the ninth story, *Planet of Giants*.

Several people, including Wilson and Newman, worked out the concepts of *Doctor Who* in the long run-up to production, and C.E. Webber – a BBC scriptwriter – formalised the results in a series of format documents. It's now uncertain who was responsible for any one idea, but Webber's early background notes mention the time machine's unreliability and the Doctor's inability to control it properly. In May 1963, Webber's briefing notes mention that any character entering the police box 'is immediately inside an extensive electronic contrivance'. 'Though it looks impressive, it is an old beat-up model, which Dr Who stole when he escaped from his own galaxy ... it is uncertain in performance and often needs repairing; moreover, Dr Who has forgotten how to work it, so they have to learn by trial and error.' The seeds of many later developments in the programme's mythology – even including the Doctor's mysterious origins – were sown here.

The briefing document was revised for potential writers by the series' first script editor, David Whitaker, who refined Donald Wilson's earliest thoughts on the TARDIS's capabilities: now, 'the "ship" may transport the four characters backwards or forwards, sideways into lesser or greater dimensions or into non-gravitational existence or invisibility etcetera.' He also added 'living quarters' to the description of the 'extensive electronic contrivance' inside the police box, as well as the 'occasional bric-a-brac acquired by the Doctor in his travels'.

In the 1960s, the BBC Design Department allocated designers to programmes on a story-by-story basis. Peter Brachacki was selected to work on *Doctor Who*'s four-part opener and was briefed by Lambert in August 1963. Although he ultimately worked on only the first episode, his lasting legacy to the series was his revolutionary and iconic TARDIS interior, which was designed by Brachacki and built by independent contractors Shawcraft Models in the space of just five weeks.

An iconic design

Peter Brachacki's design was unusually large for a television set, filling half of the programme's allocated studio floor space and reaching considerably higher than any standard studio set. It was a bright and gleaming white – which would last for much of the show's original 26-year run – with the intended futuristic sterility of the setting being counterpointed by the assorted antiques and furniture dotted around the set.

There were indented circles set into each wall, later christened 'roundels' and still a prominent feature in the 2010 version. Brachacki may have been influenced by the interlocking circular pattern on pill packets; Waris Hussein, the director of the first serial, suggested that the designer was inspired by a circular pattern in the plastic he made his models from. Budget limitations stopped these roundels being anything more than decorative, though Brachacki's initial concept was for them to flash or pulsate whenever the TARDIS was in flight. That left the column at the centre of the console as the only indication of the ship's status: a regular rise and fall meant that the

TARDIS was in motion; rotation of its internal instruments showed that the time machine was at rest and surveying its surroundings. In fact, the prop was prone to mechanical faults, and a lot of time was spent over the next few years keeping the time rotor going. This proved a perennial problem – in his last story, Tom Baker's Doctor asks, 'Have you seen the state of the time column recently?'

The console itself dominated the set. It was hexagonal, and Brachacki's theory was that the Doctor – as the craft's only pilot – should be able to reach all the controls quite easily. (This was not stated in the show, however; in fact, forty-five years later, David Tennant's Doctor would reveal that a TARDIS should ideally have a crew of six, one for each panel on the console.) The controls were selected to add to the overall impression of the weird and futuristic, with a plethora of buttons, switches, levers and gauges. This craft was high-tech, and needed to look way beyond anything a 1960s audience might be familiar with.

Above the console, for these early appearances only, was another bizarre construction – some sort of huge light, comprising concentric circles inside a large hexagonal object. This was reflected by another hexagonal motif on the floor of the set beneath the console. A possible inspiration for this was the hoist control console in the centre of the BBC TV Centre's Stage 1 scenery block. This feature of the set, however, helped make the full control room design prohibitively expensive and time-consuming to be used regularly on the show, and

it was omitted from future episodes by Brachacki's successor, Barry Newbery. Almost forty-seven years later, a version of Brachacki's light was at last reincorporated into the design of the new permanent TARDIS set in Cardiff. There was no standing set available to the 1960s production team, who had to erect and take down the whole thing before and after every scene inside the time machine. While Verity Lambert had spread the cost of the TARDIS's design and construction across an entire year's run, the full set proved too ambitious for the new weekly serial. It was quickly decided that most TARDIS scenes would be filmed using just the console and two of the walls.

As so often on *Doctor Who*, this solution actually stimulated the creative flair of the programme's makers. Right from the start, the TARDIS interior was adapted to suit the demands of each individual story or scene, expanding and contracting and taking in extra details as and when they were necessary. The second serial – *The Daleks* in late November 1963 – introduced the Fault Locator. Rarely seen again, it was the first of many short-lived innovations, invented when the story required them and then discarded. Over the years, *Doctor Who*'s own mythology took advantage of these practicalities and began to incorporate the TARDIS's changing architecture and contents into the series' storylines.

THIS ISN'T OPERATING PROPERLY

Key to the Doctor's early adventures were the TARDIS's own quirks and faults. Indeed, the Fault Locator was the largest piece of machinery in the control room at that time – a great computer bank taking up an entire wall, constantly analysing the TARDIS systems and detecting

defects in individual components. Just as important to the random nature of the TARDIS's travels, though, was the Doctor's own unfamiliarity with his machine and his inability to steer it accurately. He quite quickly admitted to Ian and Barbara that the TARDIS wasn't operating properly – 'or, rather, the code is still a secret'.

The cause of the Doctor's uncertain command of his vessel was that he was not, in fact, its true owner. He had, it later transpired, 'borrowed' the time machine when he'd decided to abscond from Gallifrey, and it seems that the only way he could gain access to a TARDIS was to take one that was in for repair. Right from the start, the Doctor was careering through time and space in an erratic ship.

The Doctor clearly found the basic operation of the TARDIS – the taking off, the landing, working the scanner and opening the doors – straightforward enough. He was able to understand the myriad dials and readouts on the console, with their measurements of gravity, atmosphere, radiation levels and other environmental conditions outside the ship. But he found that the ship's computers required twelve minutes to re-orientate and power up after a landing, and the only means of piloting the TARDIS with any precision was by inputting masses of data, including the exact time and place of departure and the coordinates from Galactic Zero Centre of the required destination. Unfortunately, the yearometer that told him when the TARDIS had landed was one of the first vital instruments to break down.

It was followed by the radiation detector, which failed to alert them to dangerous conditions on Skaro – a

THE DALEKS
by Terry Nation
Starring William Hartnell as the Doctor
First broadcast: 21/12/1963–01/02/1964

situation only exacerbated by the Doctor's rash decision to sabotage the fluid link so that he could stay and explore this new world. This led not only to the discovery that the TARDIS stores had run out of mercury, which was needed for the fluid link, but also to the time

travellers' first encounter with the Daleks. The next technical failure occurred as soon as the TARDIS left Skaro, when the Doctor pressed the Fast Return switch and it stayed pressed. This caused the TARDIS to hurtle back through time and space not to London, 1963, but to the very beginning of the universe, a space-time event that even the TARDIS could not survive.

The Doctor's understanding of his TARDIS grew throughout his first and second incarnations, although he rarely had complete control. Ironically, it was when the Time Lords caught up with him and seemingly put an end to his travels, that he finally had a chance to learn about the time machine in detail.

THE EDGE OF DESTRUCTION
by David Whitaker
Starring William Hartnell as the Doctor
First broadcast:
08/02/1964–15/02/1964

BLACK-AND-GREEN TV

In 1970, *Doctor Who*'s production moved into colour, and viewers discovered that the console was not, in fact, white. To achieve the familiar bright white appearance for black and white television, it had actually been necessary to paint the console a pale green.

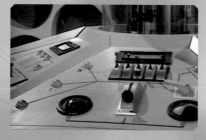

You've redecorated

The Third Doctor's exile to Earth by the Time Lords left him with time on his hands and the motivation to get his TARDIS back in full working order. He immediately discovered that, although he'd been allowed to keep the time machine, its dematerialisation codes had been changed to prevent him from operating it. Having re-established contact with Brigadier Lethbridge-Stewart, the Doctor became UNIT's unofficial, unpaid scientific adviser, in exchange for facilities and equipment to effect repairs.

The Doctor's first move was to extract the central console from the TARDIS and into the UNIT HQ laboratory, where he attempted to repair the Time Vector Generator. (Removal of this component collapsed the interior dimensions of the TARDIS, so the inside of the police box shell was presumably the size of an actual police box at this point.) He managed to briefly reactivate the device, but was caught up in its time warp field and was projected fifteen seconds into the future, along with his assistant Liz Shaw.

📺 **THE AMBASSADORS OF DEATH**
by David Whitaker
Starring Jon Pertwee
as the Doctor
First broadcast:
21/03/1970–02/05/1970

For a while, it seems, the Doctor's repairs went rather well. With Liz Shaw's assistance, he was able to identify and sort out a number of faults.

He decided to attempt an escape from Earth with just the console, using power leeched from a top-secret research project that UNIT was providing security for. An unexpected interruption in the power flow then flung the Doctor into an alternative dimension, where he found a parallel Earth with significant and dangerous differences from the one he'd just left.

The Doctor now abandoned this approach, instead unsuccessfully concentrating his efforts on fixing the ship's Mark One dematerialisation circuit, even attempting to substitute a Mark Two he'd liberated from the Master's TARDIS. Meanwhile, he restored the Time Vector Generator and returned the console to the regrown interior dimensions of the ship. The TARDIS now underwent its first spot of redecoration, probably under the Doctor's instructions, rather than of its own volition. The console in particular gave every impression of being brand new, although for a while it would be difficult to tell, since it was covered with a mass of disconnected cabling and equipment. The scanner screen was, briefly, relocated into one of the roundels on the wall.

The Doctor – or the TARDIS itself – frequently altered the appearance of these roundels and the position and appearance of the scanner throughout his third and fourth incarnations. This was a period of resumed adventure, since the Time Lords frequently took advantage of having a useful agent at large in the universe. Able to remotely control the TARDIS, they provided a new dematerialisation circuit and despatched the Doctor to deal with problematic situations on the planets Uxareius, Peladon and Solos.

IN THE STUDIO

Always adept at getting the most out of a fairly small television budget, the 1970s production team headed by producer Barry Letts often used the TARDIS set – with slight redressing – for both the Doctor's and the Master's control room, a trick revived in the 1980s for the return of the Master. This occasionally gave the impression that all renegade Time Lords not only had a synchronised impulse to redesign their TARDISes, they even shared the same designer.

The Time Lords subsequently restored the Doctor's knowledge of dematerialisation theory. The stellar engineer Omega had broken through from his antimatter universe and attempted to take revenge on the Time Lords, but the first three Doctors had united to defeat him. The Doctor's reward was the lifting of his exile, though the Time Lords continued to regard him as a useful asset, sending him to planets like Spiridon, Skaro and Karn to deal with Daleks or the mad Time Lord Morbius.

The control room remained flexible throughout this time, on one occasion even providing a wall unit with a slide-out bed for the unconscious Third Doctor. The adjacent wall at that time comprised opaque plastic windows.

After a stint in the wood-panelled Secondary Control Room (see page 52), the Fourth Doctor reopened the original. Now calling it the Number Two Control Room, he claimed it

THE SECONDARY CONTROL ROOM

For a time, the Fourth Doctor operated the TARDIS from what he initially told Sarah Jane Smith was the Secondary Control Room. (He promptly remembered that it was in fact 'the old one'.) This was a rather smaller, wood-panelled version, which the Doctor and Sarah stumbled across while wandering through the TARDIS. Wooden shutters opened to reveal the scanner. The console, like the walls, seemed to be made of wood, its six hatched panels lifting to reveal hinged compartments, like those of an old-fashioned stationery bureau.

THE MASQUE OF MANDRAGORA
by Louis Marks
Starring Tom Baker as the Doctor
First broadcast:
04/09/1976–25/09/1976

》》 *In 1976, producer Philip Hinchcliffe asked long-serving designer Barry Newbery to create a more compact control room that would occupy less studio space. Newbery took the early science-fiction writings of Jules Verne as his inspiration, basing the console on a Davenport desk and placing it in an Edwardian-looking environment. Sadly, the wood panels could not survive storage conditions between seasons, and the new look lasted only a year.*

had been closed for redecoration because he didn't like the colour. It was still white. ('That's the trouble with computers ... No imagination!') By this time, he'd also put a hat-stand in the room, usually hung with an assortment of long coats and longer scarves.

It was the Fifth Doctor who gave the TARDIS systems their next significant overhaul, reconfiguring the TARDIS console in the process. Its controls, which had developed an alarming habit of coming off in his hand, were all replaced with touch-sensitive buttons, and its dials and readouts were updated, with computerised displays replacing ticker-tape printouts. Despite this, the TARDIS remained unpredictable, though the Doctor was by now increasingly confident in his control of the time machine, getting better at short hops and sometimes even managing to reach his intended destination.

Low-Tech?

At some point towards the end of his seventh life, the Doctor dramatically reconfigured the control room. It now bore some resemblance to the wood-panelled version briefly used by the Fourth Doctor, but was much, much larger. No longer a brightly lit and sterile environment from the distant future, it was redolent of some ancient cathedral, its redwood walls, balconies, stairways, columns and pylons all crested with the Seal of Rassilon – a Time Lord emblem that perhaps indicated a softening in the Doctor's attitude towards his people and his heritage. But this grand alien space was also full of the trappings of late nineteenth- or early twentieth-century English culture – the library, the comfortable armchair, the outdated gramophone, the antique timepieces, all reminders of the Doctor's favourite planet.

DOCTOR WHO
by Matthew Jacobs
Starring Paul McGann
and Sylvester McCoy
as the Doctor
First UK broadcast:
27/05/1996

At its heart, of course, lay the hexagonal console, again a wooden construction adorned with old-fashioned gauges and dials and gold-plated switches and levers, but much larger than previously seen. The column at the console's centre rose to a vast domed ceiling, which acted as a huge scanner, showing anything from the immediate environment outside the ship to dramatic displays of entire star systems and galaxies. A separate monitor screen could be pulled towards the console on a flexible spring, and on it was displayed the TARDIS's temporal and physical status.

```
INT. THE TARDIS

Coming off a close-up reaction shot on Lee, we see a vast
space with the master control console in the centre. Lee
moves right inside, almost to the console, awestruck by the
size of the place. The only light seems to come from outside.
Suddenly, the door slams shut behind us and we are plunged
into near-darkness. Lee peers back into the echoing shadows,
sensing movement but unable to see.

                    LEE
        Who's there?

Then, as if in response, the Master's
evil eyes glow back at him through the
dark and the Master sweeps towards him.

                  MASTER
        You don't want to know.
```

DOCTOR WHO
by Matthew Jacobs

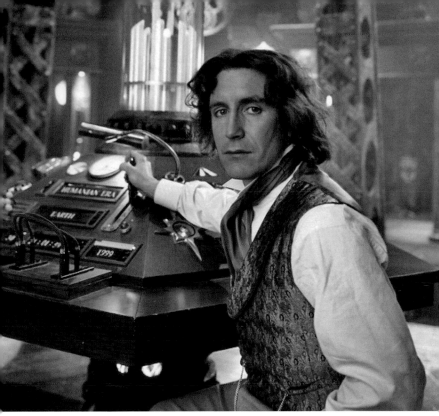

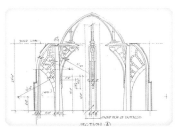

RESTORATION

The control room and console built for *The Five Doctors* in 1983 lasted until the end of the series' original run in December 1989. When *Doctor Who* returned – for one night only – in 1996, it was as a lavish UK-US co-production, an 85-minute TV movie with a budget far in excess of anything the programme had known before. With the possibility of an ongoing US-based series, the Executive Producer Philip Segal was determined that every aspect of the movie would show off the visual potential of *Doctor Who*. Large parts of the script were set inside the time machine, including the opening scenes and the climax, so the large-scale and entirely redesigned TARDIS interior was the production's centrepiece.

Production Designer Richard Hudolin brought a fresh perspective to the familiar iconic elements of the original control room. Hudolin combined wood and brass fixtures and fittings with a network of tall pylons and an arched ceiling to produce a cavernous interior with a Victorian flavour. The intricate design – inspired by a seashell – was carefully proportioned so that all points in it were equidistant from each other. The roundels were no longer simply impressions in the walls – their shapes were cut out of the columns and pylons, which allowed Director Geoffrey Sax to shoot a far greater variety of shots than had ever been possible in the old two- or three-wall set.

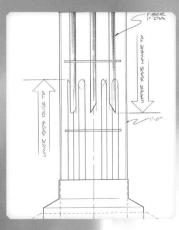

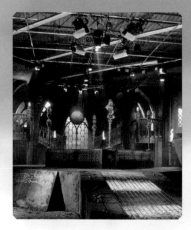

SURVIVOR OF THE TIME WAR

Attacked by shop-window dummies in the basement of a department store, 19-year-old Rose Tyler was saved by the mysterious Doctor, who told her he was there to stop an alien invasion. Rose's instinctive doubts were stripped away when she found herself facing a plastic replica of her boyfriend Mickey and was then chased by its headless body – straight inside a wooden box.

In a blind panic, Rose runs
into the box –

INT. TARDIS Night 2 continuous

– into a big, wide, wonderful
room. ROSE stops dead. THE
DOCTOR's far away, busy at a
central six-sided console,
which is a jam of all sorts
of technology, big old 60s' buttons and
futuristic devices. And around that, high above, the
shine of epic, alien design, the whole place humming with
suppressed energy.

ROSE
by Russell T Davies

The box, of course, was the TARDIS. But this was a TARDIS that had, alongside the Doctor, survived a dreadful Time War. Gallifrey had gone, the Time Lords had gone, even the Daleks had apparently gone. The only survivors were the regenerated Ninth Doctor and his time machine.

Like the Doctor, the TARDIS interior itself had changed dramatically. Still an impossibly huge space, it now looked impossibly old, too. The gleaming technacothaka was long gone, replaced with buttresses and panels of coral-encrusted wood and ceramic, with a bizarre array of quite ordinary objects in place of switches and buttons – as if this advanced alien machinery had been patched up using the contents of a junkyard. A battered pilot's seat was bolted to the metal floor near one panel on the console, and the glass column at the machine's centre was festooned with cables stretching off to all corners of the room. A hat stand stood near the police box doors that led back outside the TARDIS.

ROSE
by Russell T Davies
Starring Christopher Eccleston as the Doctor
First UK broadcast: 26/03/2005

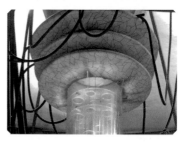

EVOLUTION

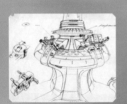

When *Doctor Who* returned in 2005 as a BBC Wales production, a fifty-strong team was assembled by Production Designer Edward Thomas. Edward coordinates the Art Department and ensures a consistent visual feel to every episode, with one of the most significant elements being, of course, the TARDIS itself. The idea was that the new-look *Doctor Who* should be, at every level, an evolution from what had gone before, and the new TARDIS was the most effective symbol of that. Edward decided that the interior would have an organic appearance – that a TARDIS was, in fact, grown and not built. (These design ideas later fed into the script for *The Impossible Planet*, when the Doctor told Rose that TARDISes were grown.)

Edward and artist Bryan Hitch worked out some initial ideas about this organic feel, which concept designers Dan Walker and Matthew Savage then developed further. Edward was keen that everything should be constructed from natural materials, so everything was made from (or looked like it was made from) wood, glass or coral. It was Dan's idea that the console should flow into the curved floor, ceiling and walls, while Matthew worked on incorporating the roundels into the

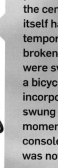

design. These he placed inside hexagonal devices throughout the TARDIS interior. And the inside of the police box doors stood at the entrance to the set, a quiet echo of two 1960s films starring Peter Cushing as Dr Who.

The console had a ceramic surround, and the overall impression was of a machine that had changed and evolved over its 900 years – it had taken a bit of a battering over the centuries. Both the Doctor and the TARDIS itself had scavenged through the universe for temporary replacements when controls had broken or worn out. Buttons and switches were swapped for things like chess pieces; a bicycle pump and a handbrake were incorporated into the machinery; a hammer swung from the side of the console for those moments when the Doctor needed to give the console an encouraging thump. The TARDIS was now a real amalgamation of different ages, styles and technologies.

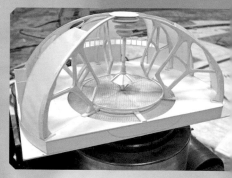

Based on the concept artwork and 3D model shown on the preceding pages, construction began in Newport in summer 2004.

The shell was made of steel and rose to a height of 10.5 metres (35 feet)...

One side of the control room set was open to the rest of the studio floor.

... so the set-builders needed cranes to dress the highest points.

The police box doors seen to the left of the control room shell.

The core of the central console, prior to dressing.

OH, YOU SEXY THING!

The Tenth Doctor's explosive regeneration (see page 111) was almost the end of the TARDIS. The regeneration energy pouring out of him wreaked havoc around the control room, blazing into the console and shattering the police box windows. As flames erupted around the console, buttresses crashed to the floor and debris cascaded from the huge domed ceiling. Moments later, the new – Eleventh – Doctor was born among the wreckage, only to find that his ship was crashing towards planet Earth.

It landed in Amelia Pond's back garden (see page 17). But while the Doctor was examining the crack in Amelia's bedroom wall, the TARDIS engines were phasing – the Doctor was forced to take a quick trip into the future to stabilise them. The five-minute trip took twelve years, of course, but it did the trick, and the Doctor left his ship to regenerate itself while he and Amy took on Prisoner Zero and the Atraxi. But he knew that the TARDIS would alert him when its own regeneration was complete...

On the Doctor, also watching – and then wincing in pain. He reaches into his pocket and pulls out:

The TARDIS key.

(FX) It's glowing – fiercely and rhythmically, like a signal.

On Amy, still staring.

               AMY
So is that it? Is that them gone for good? Who were they?

She turns to look at the Doctor –

THE ELEVENTH HOUR
by Steven Moffat

– and he's gone.

EVOLUTION

Edward Thomas's 2010 redesign began life as a computer-generated 3D model, allowing views of every aspect of the new interior from any angle.

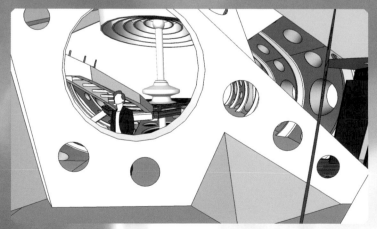

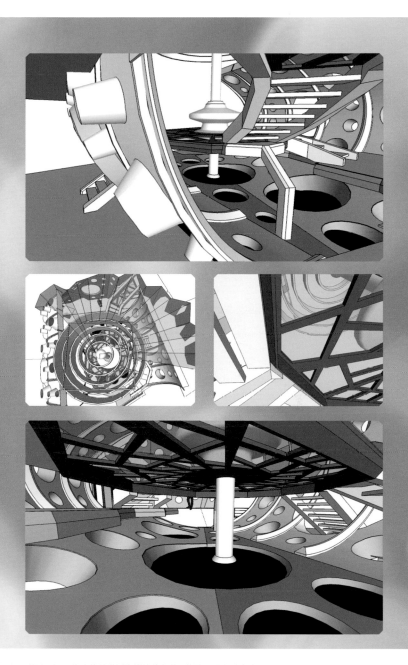

Edward Thomas and designers James North and Peter McKinstry have conceptually based the latest TARDIS redesign on a romantic notion of a ship voyaging through time. The undulating shape of the walls and floor are an echo of the waves of time that the TARDIS surfs in its travels. The copper and brass and wood of the fittings are reminiscent of an Edwardian seafaring craft, and many of the console's instruments are themselves lifted from just such a vessel – the sextant, the compass, the pressure gauges – all designed to give a maritime effect. This is capped by the new lamp on the police box exterior, salvaged from a naval ship. They've stopped short of sticking barnacles around the console, but that weather-beaten effect has been painstakingly achieved. Everywhere, there is a finish of malachite – a greenish crystalline copper carbonate caused by the weathering of the metal fixtures. There's a whole new level beneath that glass floor, and another up a flight of stairs with mysterious doors leading to who knows where. Off to one side, beyond the brass rails, down the steps, are those police box doors.

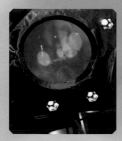

As with its most recent previous incarnation, there is an air of the scavenger about this control room. Where you might expect glittering buttons and digital displays, there are dozens of archaic fragments of salvaged equipment. Computer keyboard nestles near rusty typewriter, an old telephone and a cassette deck. Several of these bear the logo 'Magpie Electricals', a reminder of recent adventures. At the base of the console, drum pedals and footbrakes rest on the polished glass floor – put in specially for one-time footballer Matt Smith to have something to do with his feet. Each panel of the console has been carefully allocated a function by the Art Department, as shown on the next three pages.

INT. TARDIS — DAY

The phone on the console, ringing.

              AMY
People phone you?

              THE DOCTOR
    (Busy at the console)
It's a phone box. Would you
mind?

              AMY
    (Answering phone)
Hello? Sorry, who? No,
seriously, who?
    (To the Doctor)
Says he's the Prime Minister.

HELM

Steering mechanism

Eyepiece

Time rotor handbrake

NAVIGATION

Directional pointer

Atom accelerator

Time and space
forward/back control

DIAGNOSTIC

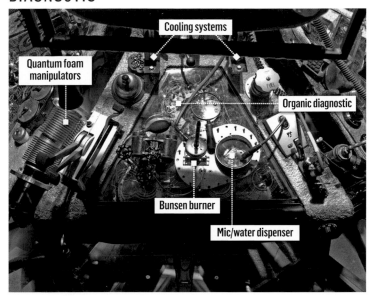

Cooling systems

Quantum foam manipulators

Organic diagnostic

Bunsen burner

Mic/water dispenser

COMMUNICATIONS

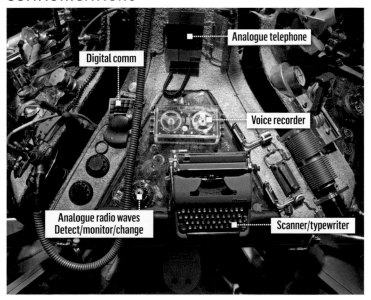

Analogue telephone

Digital comm

Voice recorder

Analogue radio waves Detect/monitor/change

Scanner/typewriter

FABRICATION

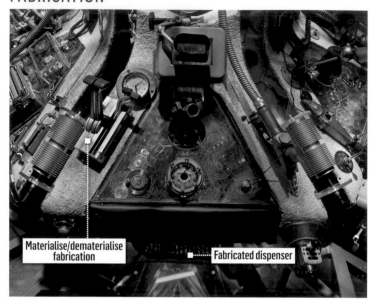

Materialise/dematerialise fabrication

Fabricated dispenser

MECHANICAL

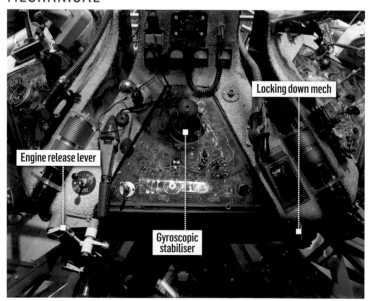

Locking down mech

Engine release lever

Gyroscopic stabiliser

3

IN FLIGHT

T he days of the Doctor being unable to fly the TARDIS accurately are long gone. Things improved dramatically after the Third Doctor took everything apart and put most of it back together again, and the Fourth Doctor was generally able to steer his craft with reasonable accuracy, as were his successors. The Ninth Doctor was even able to pilot the

TARDIS through a Dalek fleet of 200 vessels, landing on the Command Deck of the Dalek Emperor's saucer with absolute precision to rescue Rose Tyler.

Faced with a revived Dalek menace to Earth, the new Doctor exceeds even that feat, taking the TARDIS from wartime England straight into the main chamber of another

huge spaceship, and managing to materialise apparently unnoticed in the midst of three Daleks. But the Doctor is unable to prevent these Daleks from activating their Progenitor device, and an entirely new – and pure – race of Daleks is soon brought into being.

VICTORY OF THE DALEKS
by Mark Gatiss
Starring Matt Smith as the Doctor
First broadcast: 17/04/2010

JOURNEY LOG
Victory of the Daleks

Professor Edwin Bracewell, a Scottish-born scientist, was delighted to find revolutionary new ideas simply popping into his head: hypersonic flight, gravity bubbles... and the Ironsides: khaki-coloured robots, capable of entirely independent function, utterly devoted to winning the war, armed with deadly laser weaponry, and recognised only by the Doctor. They

are in fact just one part of a Dalek scheme to entrap the Doctor and use him to convince a recovered Progenitor device of their Dalek heritage. It's not Churchill's war that the Daleks are determined to win...

Winston Churchill

Prime Minister of the United Kingdom during the Second World War, Churchill led the fight against the Nazi occupation of Europe. He was prepared to condone almost anything that would bring victory a little closer, even deploying a new form of fighting machine which would, he was sure, win the war. Enthusiastic as he was about his new secret weapon, however, Churchill was also cautious enough to request advice from a trusted friend – the Doctor.

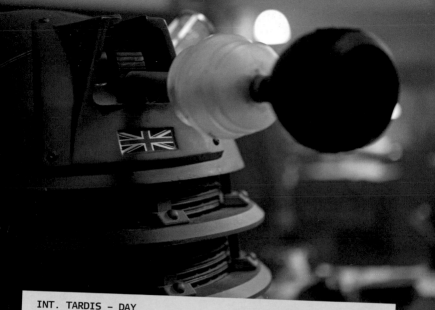

INT. TARDIS - DAY

THE DOCTOR's all over the controls. Information pours
across screens on the console.

FX: CLOSE on screen: Earth. Then Earth in space. A grid
shimmering over the image. And there, hanging in the
blackness, the Enemy ship.

                          THE DOCTOR
    Bingo!

He flicks a switch.

VICTORY OF THE DALEKS
by Mark Gatiss

The Crooked Smile

Though he's too busy dealing with the Daleks to find out more about it,
the Doctor is shocked to discover that Amy – a girl from the year 2010 –
has no idea what Daleks are. The removal of planet Earth to the Medusa
Cascade and the subsequent Dalek invasion are just not events that she
could have forgotten. Yet Amy has never heard of Daleks. Could it have
anything to do with the huge crack in the wall of Churchill's War Room?

Just like the split in reality that the
Doctor closed when he and Amy first
met... the crooked smile that was
replicated on the TARDIS scanner
screen as she joined him in the
TARDIS... and just the same as the
crack in the hull of Starship UK...

New Daleks!

Dalek Progenitor devices were scattered through the universe before the Time War, each containing the seed of the Daleks – the possibility of resurrecting their species. Now the Ironsides' complex plan to effect the reactivation of the Progenitor reaches fruition, and the Doctor is faced with the first of a new Dalek army. Bigger than they have ever been and resplendent in multicoloured livery, these Daleks represent every aspect of a new and invincible Dalek race.

ETERNAL   DRONE   SUPREME   SCIENTIST   STRATEGIST

HOLD THAT ONE DOWN

The Doctor has used, mentioned, disregarded, repaired or discarded many different TARDIS components, processes and functions in 900 years of phone-box travel. He's patched up, replaced or stolen components from other Time Lords' TARDISes. His explanations of what they actually do, when he's bothered to explain at all, have only occasionally made sense to his human companions. He's sometimes been known to refer to some of the same components by different names. The Doctor has rarely been too concerned with getting the details right...

Analogue/Radio-Wave detector: Feature of the regenerated console. (2010)

Analogue telephone: Winston Churchill's call to the Doctor came through on this. (2010)

Astral Map: Removable equipment, used to plot the Menoptra approach to Vortis and to monitor their communications. Also used to calculate the remaining life of a dying planet in Galaxy 4. (1965)

Astro-Sextant Rectifier: Went out of phase when the TARDIS collided with the Mandragora Helix. (1976)

Atmospheric Excitation: Produced snowfall outside the TARDIS. (2006)

Atom Accelerator: Feature of the regenerated console. (2010)

Automatic Drift Control: Added to the Mark IV Type 40, it allowed a TARDIS to be safely suspended in space. (1965)

Automatic Emergency Landing: Instigated after critical timing malfunction caused by the Master invading TARDIS systems. (1996)

Automatic Oxygen Supply: Ran out on Spiridon when fungoid spores sealed TARDIS doors. (1973)

Bunsen Burner: Feature of the regenerated console. (2010)

Calibrators: Were on the blink when the TARDIS landed on Karn. (1976)

Chameleon Arch: Rewrote the Doctor's biology from Gallifreyan to human. (2007)

Chameleon Circuit: See page 20

Cloister Bell: Communications device warning of wild catastrophes. (1981)

Communications Circuit: The Doctor boosted the Brigadier's walkie-talkie through this to contact troops outside UNIT HQ. (1973)

Comparator: Removed to immobilise TARDIS. (1984)

Complete Systems Shutdown: Initiated by the Doctor prior to attempting to submerse the TARDIS in the River Thames. (1981)

Conceptual Geometer: The TARDIS had to be shut down before attempting modifications to this. (1980)

Cooling Systems: Feature of the regenerated console. (2010)

Deep Scan Control: Activated while the Doctor traced and trapped a 'ghost'. (2006)

Defence Shield, Primary: Linking the primary and secondary TARDIS circuits to this, the Doctor and Time Lord technician Rodan managed to switch control of Gallifrey's transduction barriers to the TARDIS, preventing a large-scale Sontaran invasion. (1978) The shield was extended outside the ship to form a safe passage from the exterior doors to a nearby Skonnon spaceship. (1980)

Dematerialisation Circuit: Rendered inactive by the Time Lords at the start of the Doctor's Earth exile, but vital to TARDIS operation. (1971)

Dematerialisation Systems: One of the six control panels on the console.

Digital Comms: Feature of the regenerated console. (2010)

Digital disc player: The Doctor played an Ian Dury and the Blockheads CD on this; (2006) it was also able to read an authorised control disc. (2007)

Dimensional Control Unit/Dimension Circuits: The Doctor removed this from the Monk's TARDIS, causing the interior dimensions to compress. (1965) The circuits in the Master's TARDIS were affected by his own Tissue Compression Eliminator device. (1983) See also Time Vector Generator.

Directional Pointer: Feature of the regenerated console. (2010)

Directional Unit: Necessary for accurate piloting of a TARDIS; the Doctor stole an incompatible one from the Monk's TARDIS to use in his own, but it burnt out after only one journey. (1965)

Door control: At various times a switch or a large, red-topped lever on the console; eventually superseded by an Era-make latch on the inside of the external door.

Drift Compensators: Needed setting after the TARDIS arrived on Nerva Beacon to prevent the ship slipping off. (1975)

Dynomorphic Generators: When these were exhausted, the Master's TARDIS was stranded in Earth's Jurassic period. (1982)

Dynomorphic Regenerator: Used to regenerate Dynomorphic Generators. (1982)

Emergency Bypass: Used to restore an unstable interface between the TARDIS and a nearby spacecraft. (1983)

Emergency door control: A manual winding key used to open the doors when the TARDIS suffered a power failure on Exilon. (1974) The Doctor had previously used unspecified energy from a ring to open the doors during a similar loss of power and control over the TARDIS. (1965)

Emergency Instructions: The TARDIS data banks contained 18,348 of these. (1980)

Emergency Oxygen Supply: Bank of oxygen cylinders which ran out on Spiridon when fungoid spores sealed the TARDIS doors. (1973)

Emergency Power: Form of systems standby that sheltered the TARDIS from detection. (2007)

Emergency Power Booster: Used in bid to escape white void beyond reality. (1968) The last vestiges of emergency power were used to get the TARDIS to Varos for Zeiton 7 ore. (1985)

Emergency Program One: Activated when the Doctor faces an enemy that must never get hold of a TARDIS; it returned Rose home during the Dalek attack of 200,100. (2005)

Emergency Storage Cells: Activated in case of power failure, but drained by the Exxilon City. (1974)

Emergency Transceiver (Mark III): Disconnected by the Doctor because he kept getting calls from Gallifrey, this sent and received distress signals. (1980)

Emergency Unit: Activated to escape the lava flow of an erupting volcano, it removed the TARDIS from space-time. (1968)

Engine Release Lever: Feature of the regenerated console. (2010)

Exterior Monitor: One of the six control panels on the console.

Extreme Emergency Switch: Operated by Jo Grant to retrieve the Doctor from the Time Vortex. (1972)

Eye of Harmony: The Time Lords' power source on Gallifrey; a part or copy of it – or a link to it – was inside each TARDIS, fuelling the time ships; the Master opened it on Earth and dangerously changed the molecular structure of the planet. (1996) After the destruction of Gallifrey, the Doctor's TARDIS needed an alternative fuel source, such as the Cardiff Rift. (2005)

Eyepiece: Feature of the regenerated console. (2010)

Fabricated Dispenser: Feature of the regenerated console. (2010)

Failsafe: Operated by pulling a switch just beyond the control room's internal door, this put the TARDIS in a fixed temporal and physical state for eternity (or until the switch was flicked back). This saved the TARDIS from being plunged into a black hole when

Kelner reversed the stabiliser banks in Gallifrey's Capitol. (1978)

Fast Return Switch: Means of effecting a swift reverse journey; this once jammed, sending the TARDIS back to the start of the universe. (1964)

Fault Locator: Computer bank monitoring and analysing defects in TARDIS systems; (1963) now superseded by small device on regenerated console. (2010)

Flight computer: Still recently regenerated, the Sixth Doctor wiped its memory while carrying out repairs. (1985)

Fluid Links (K7): Console component requiring supply of liquid mercury. It was sabotaged by the Doctor so he could explore Skaro. (1963) It once shattered, flooding the control room with mercury vapour and forcing the evacuation of the TARDIS, and later could not withstand the pressure of escaping a volcanic lava flow, threatening to fill the control room with mercury again. (1968)

Food machine: This stood in an alcove off the control room, and dispensed solid cubes flavoured according to the user's selection. (1963)

Force Barrier/Force Field: This has easily withstood firepower from, among many others, Rills and Daleks. (1965) It was briefly neutralised by the Monk. (1966) It had to be switched off to allow telepathic communication between the Doctor in the TARDIS and the Mentiads on Zanak. (1978)

Force-Field Generator: Contained behind a panel in the base of a console, the Second and Third Doctors sacrificed this (and the Second's recorder) to defeat Omega. (1973)

Gravitic Anomaliser: A hasty stand-in for the immobilised dimensional stabiliser, with mixed results, before being used to repair a stranded Skonnon spacecraft and a Nimon capsule. (1980)

Gravity Dilation Meter: Manned by Romana during the Doctor's successful attempt to prevent the pirate planet Zanak from materialising around the Earth. (1978)

Gravity Tractor Beam: Used variously to hold back a neutron star, (1980) tow the Sanctuary Base rocket away from a black hole, (2006) and pull planet Earth from the Medusa Cascade to its home system. (2008)

Gyroscopic Stabiliser: Feature of the regenerated console. (2010)

Helmic Regulator: Given quite a twist by Harry Sullivan, this sent the TARDIS thousands of years into the future to Space Station Nerva. (1975) The Doctor fired it up as part of the dematerialisation process, (2007) and floored it when escaping a time crash with an earlier TARDIS. (2008)

Home Box: Similar to an aeroplane's black box, a Home Box records its ship's flight data and takes it home if anything happens to the ship. River Song left a message for the Doctor in Old High Gallifreyan on one, which he linked into the TARDIS systems in order to reach River on the *Byzantium*. (2010)

Hostile Action Displacement System (HADS):
Detected external danger and removed the TARDIS to the nearest safe location. (1968)

Hover Mode: The Doctor advised Nyssa to put the TARDIS into hover mode while escaping Event One. (1982)

Huon Particles: A remnant of Huon energy, a dangerous power source eliminated by the Time Lords, lies at the heart of the TARDIS. (2006)

Image Translator: A key component of the TARDIS scanner, it reads the absolute value of the time machine's landing coordinates and converts them into an image on the screen of what is outside the ship. (1980)

Information System: Data store and full manual accessible via a monitor screen and keyboard on the console. (1982)

Internal Systems: One of the six control panels on the console.

Interstitial Beam Synthesizer: A fault in this caused the TARDIS scanner to malfunction after materialisation on the planet Peladon. (1972)

Journey log: A device recording details of each place and time period the TARDIS visited. Its records were played back on the scanner as the TARDIS sped back to the start of the universe. (1964)

Key to Time Tracer Core: Given to Romana by the White Guardian, the tracer located segments of the Key to Time and, in contact with them, converted them back from their disguises. It plugged into a newly drilled hole in the TARDIS console and could guide the ship to each of six locations and time zones to find the segments. (1978)

Lateral Balance Cones: Played up during an attempt to pilot the TARDIS to Heathrow in 1981. (1982)

Light-Speed Overdrive: Malfunctioning component of the Doctor's TARDIS; the working component from the Master's TARDIS linked in to the Pharos Project systems on Earth to project data into space and prevent a CVE from closing, so saving the universe from heat death. (1981)

Linear Calculator: Not performing correctly, this may have caused the TARDIS to land on the planet Oseidon while en route to Earth. (1975)

Lockdown Mechanism: Feature of the regenerated console. (2010)

Magnetic Card Reader: Device on TARDIS console that supplied ticker-tape printouts of ancient data stored on magnetic card, e.g. the Record of Rassilon. (1980)

Manual Override: Put all TARDIS systems under manual control while attempting to escape Event One. (1982)

Master Control: One of the six control panels on the console.

Materialisation Fabrication: Feature of the regenerated console. (2010)

Materialisation Field: Jammed when the TARDIS and the pirate planet Zanak attempted a simultaneous materialisation around the planet Calufrax. (1978)

Materialisation Flip-Flop: Emergency manoeuvre performed by the Fifth Doctor to evade the Sentinel Six defence satellite. (1984)

Mean-Free Path-Tracker: Component of the TARDIS console speculatively identified by Nyssa of Traken. (1982)

Microphone: Feature of the regenerated console. (2010)

Mobile phone: Martha Jones gave the Doctor her phone when she left the TARDIS, and he kept it on the console. Martha used it to request his help with the Sontarans' ATMOS system, and she and other companions called it via a Subwave Network after the Daleks stole planet Earth. (2008)

Molecular Stabilisers: Component of all Type 40 TARDISes, used to regenerate K-9's systems after an attack by the Ogri. (1978)

Monitor screen: Part of the console, this displayed the Master's fictional 'TARDIS Index File' to Nyssa and Tegan. (1982) It was used to chart a route through Gallifrey's Death Zone to the Dark Tower, (1983) and could plot the course of a time corridor. (1984) It was mounted on a Z-spring in the Eighth Doctor's control room and used to report the ship's status. (1996) Seemingly cannibalised from a 21st-century computer monitor, it combined these functions with local TV reception and the scanner utility in the Ninth and Tenth Doctors' control room (2005) and could be synchronised with the large wall-scanner in the Eleventh Doctor's TARDIS. (2010)

Multi-Loop Stabiliser: Essential to a smooth materialisation, according to the TARDIS instruction manual, but unused by the Doctor. (1978)

Navigation Control: One of the six control panels on the console.

Navigational System: The Doctor sabotaged this part of the Rani's TARDIS to trap her and the Master. (1987)

Omega Configuration, folding back: First stage in Complete Systems Shutdown. (1981)

Organic Diagnostic: Feature of the regenerated console. (2010)

Oxygen masks: These drop down from above the console during an emergency or crash-landing. (2006)

Pause Control: Facility that allows the TARDIS to materialise temporarily in one location before continuing on a programmed journey. Could be activated by leaving the key in the exterior lock, probably thanks to a fault. (1975)

Power cell: The last glimmer of energy in the dead TARDIS after it crashed through the Void to land on a parallel Earth. The Doctor charged it up with his own energy, and used it as a weapon to disable some Cybermen. (2006)

Quantum Accelerator: Component exchanged with the Master for a Temporal Limiter. (1982)

Quantum Foam Manipulators: Feature of the regenerated console. (2010)

Radiation detector: Console-mounted gauge which failed when the TARDIS first landed on Skaro. (1963)

Randomiser: Device fitted to the console by the Doctor to introduce a (further) element of pot luck to the navigation systems and prevent the Black Guardian tracking the TARDIS. (1979) The Doctor disabled or bypassed it several times before cannibalising it to create a random field frame in an Argolin Tachyon Recreation Generator. (1980)

Recall Circuit: Part of the Space-Time Element, this now-defunct component was used to recall the TARDIS to Gallifrey, once by the Master (1976) and once by the Time Lord High Council. (1983) This is a summons that cannot be refused, in contrast with, e.g., the message calling Romana back to Gallifrey. (1980)

Record of Rassilon: The Time Lords' official account of their war against the Great Vampires, including a command to every Time Lord to fight any surviving Vampires and vague details of how to destroy one; it was kept on a magnetic card storage system and held by every Type 40 TARDIS. (1980)

Referential Differencer: Component of the TARDIS console speculatively identified by Nyssa of Traken. (1982)

Relative Continuum Stabiliser: Its failure may have allowed, or been caused by, a projection of the Osiran Sutekh into the TARDIS control room. (1975)

Relative Dimensional Stabiliser: The Doctor removed this from the TARDIS and used it to miniaturise clones of himself and Leela while combating a microscopic viral nucleus. (1977) It is an integral part of the materialisation process, and is the source of the noise the TARDIS makes when landing or taking off, as heard by the Minyan crew of the R1C. (1978)

Relative Dimensional Stabiliser Field: Prevented a staser weapon from working inside the TARDIS. (1978)

Reverse Bias: Operating this during full flight would have disastrous consequences. (1981)

Scanner: Monitor screen displaying the environment immediately surrounding the materialised TARDIS. Located in various positions on and around the console, its earliest form resembled a television set mounted on the control room wall, at which time it received a live feed from a camera mounted on the police box roof outside. Since the TARDIS's latest regeneration, there has been a large area of one wall functioning as a circular scanner screen, with a smaller, monitor-type screen mounted on the console.

Scanner audio circuits: Repaired by the Doctor and Nyssa shortly before the TARDIS runs into the Arc of Infinity. (1983)

Seatbelts: The Doctor, Peri and H.G. Wells used seatbelts fitted to the console to ride out turbulence. (1985)

Security Protocol 712: Prompted by the presence in the TARDIS of an Authorised Control Disc, this activated a hologram of the Doctor and initiated a dematerialisation that rescued the Doctor and Martha after they had been attacked by Weeping Angels. (2007)

Self-Destruct: A 20-second countdown to the obliteration of the TARDIS, which may in fact have been a bluff by the Doctor. (1985)

Sextant: Feature of the console in the Ninth, Tenth (2005) and Eleventh (2010) Doctors' control rooms.

Signal Conversion Unit: Locked on to the frequency of the psychic energy feeding the Malus, which had invaded the TARDIS, and blocked it, causing the creature to die. (1984)

Sonic Beam: See Space-Time Telegraph.

Space-Time Coordinate Programmer: Nearly worn out by the time of the Doctor's first visit to Metebelis Three. (1973) He wired that planet's coordinates into the programmer, so was able to make two return trips to rescue Sarah Jane Smith and defeat the Giant Spiders. (1974)

Space-Time Element: The Chancellery Guard disconnected this from the console, incapacitating the TARDIS, when the Doctor was summoned to Gallifrey after Omega's second attempt to return to this universe. Another, perhaps subsidiary, element was removed from behind a roundel by Turlough, under instruction from the Black Guardian, with similar effect. (1983)

Space-Time Telegraph: Interstellar signalling device, allowing communication via a Sonic Beam. When he left UNIT soon after his third regeneration, the Doctor left a transceiver for the Brigadier to contact him in a dire emergency; when the Zygons used their Skarasen to attack North Sea oil rigs, UNIT recalled the Doctor. The receiver in the TARDIS produced a paper printout of the Brigadier's message. (1975) Winston Churchill seems to have been given a similar means of contacting the Doctor. (2010)

Stattenheim Remote Control: First seen in the hands of the Rani, who claimed to have invented it, this was a means of remote-operating a TARDIS. The Sixth Doctor had always wanted one, but the Second Doctor was actually given one by the Time Lords during a mission to prevent dangerous time-travel experiments. (1985)

Steering mechanism: Feature of the regenerated console. (2010)

Sump Flush: Feature of the regenerated console. (2010)

Synchronic Feedback-Checking Circuit: Essential to a smooth materialisation, according to the TARDIS instruction manual, but unused by the Doctor. (1978)

Tachoid Time Crystal: The Doctor informed the Kastrian Eldrad that mis-set coordinates would cause symbolic resonance in the tachoid time crystal, ending any prospect of ever rematerialising anywhere. (1976)

Telepathic Circuits: The Doctor used these to relay

his thoughts to Jo Grant when he was stranded in the Time Vortex, (1972) and to ask the Time Lords to help him find a Dalek taskforce. (1973)

Telepathic Field: The TARDIS generates a low-intensity telepathic field, which translates alien languages for its occupants. The Fourth Doctor once described it as a 'Time Lord gift I allow you to share', and told Leela that her primitive thought patterns appealed to it. (1977)

Temporal Grace, State of: Prevented use of weapons inside the TARDIS, (1976) possibly as a property of the Relative Dimensional Stabiliser Field. It failed during an assault on the TARDIS by the Cybermen. (1982)

Temporal Limiter: Component exchanged with the Master for a Quantum Accelerator. (1982)

Temporal Orbit: The TARDIS entered Temporal Orbit at the climax of the Doctor's battle with the Master in San Francisco. (1996)

Temporal Stabiliser: Component removed from the TARDIS by Kamelion, rendering it inoperable. (1984)

Thermal Buffer/Thermobuffer: The Doctor explained how to vent this while escaping Event One, (1982) and vented it when escaping a time crash with an earlier TARDIS. (2008)

Thermal Couplings: Needed fixing after a trip to the ice-cold planet Kastria. (1976)

Time & Space Forward/Backward Control: Feature of the regenerated console. (2010)

Time Controller: Removed from the TARDIS and used to send the Osiran Sutekh to his death in the distant future. (1975)

Time-Path Detector/Time-Curve Indicator: Instrument, which the Doctor implied he constructed, on the TARDIS console that displayed the progress of a pursuing Dalek time machine. (1965) Later used to detect another time machine, the Monk's TARDIS, travelling on the same course. (1966)

Time Rotor/Time Column: The cylinder rising from the centre of the console. Its rise and fall indicates that the TARDIS is in flight. There was also an instrument on the original console that measured the progress of the rotor itself. (1965)

Time Rotor Handbrake: Feature of the console in the Ninth, Tenth and Eleventh Doctors' control rooms. (2005/2010)

Time Sensor: Device constructed by the Doctor to detect disturbances in the time field, which would reveal the presence of a time machine. One was installed in the TARDIS and a second in the Doctor's car, Bessie. (1972)

Time Vector Generator: Maintains the interior dimensions of the TARDIS and is a powerful energy source. Having removed it from the TARDIS, the Doctor was able to use it as a weapon against the Cybermen. (1968) He repaired it during his exile on Earth. (1970)

Time Vortex Control: Feature of the console in the

Ninth and Tenth Doctor's control room. (2005)

Tracking equipment: By connecting the head of a Nestene replica to the console, the Doctor was able to find the source of the signal controlling the Autons. (2005)

Transitional Elements: Part of the Transpower System that marooned the TARDIS between Cetes and Scalpor when it stopped generating energy. (1985)

Transpower System: This system required the mineral ore Zeiton 7 from the planet Varos to function. (1985)

Translation Circuit: Presumably part of or connected to the Telepathic Field that translates alien languages.

Tribophysical Waveform Macro-Kinetic Extrapolator: Incorporated into the TARDIS systems as a power source and as the heart of a defence shield. (2005) Subsequently used to bump the TARDIS off course and avoid being dragged back to the Racnoss' underground lair. (2006)

Trimphone: Feature of the console in the Ninth and Tenth Doctors' control room, and used to call Rose after the defeat of the Slitheen. (2005)

Typewriter: Feature of the regenerated console. (2010)

Vector Tracker: Control on console in the Ninth and Tenth Doctors' control room. (2005)

Velocity Regulator: The Doctor sabotaged this part of the Rani's TARDIS to trap her and the Master. (1987)

Visual Stabiliser: When the Doctor removed this damaged component, the TARDIS exterior became invisible. (1968)

Voice Recorder: Feature of the regenerated console. (2010)

Vortex Drive: Used by the Doctor to generate an anti-gravity spiral and rescue a stricken spaceship disguised as a coach. (1987)

Vortex Loop: Component resembling a bicycle pump on the console in the Ninth and Tenth Doctors' control room. (2005)

Warp Drive: Among the many TARDIS systems vital to interstellar travel. (2006)

Warp Ellipse Cut-out: Process used by the Doctor to escape a time loop. (1983)

Warp Oscilloscope: Manned by Romana during the Doctor's successful attempt to prevent the pirate planet Zanak from materialising around the Earth. (1978)

Water Dispenser: Feature of the regenerated console. (2010)

Wormhole Refractors: Among the many TARDIS systems vital to interstellar travel. (2006)

Yearometer: Malfunctioning instrument on the console for calculating the time period the TARDIS had landed in. It read zero following the TARDIS's departure from 1963, and the Doctor never mentioned it again. (1963)

DOING IT BY THE BOOK

Strangely, given his longstanding difficulties handling his TARDIS, the Doctor never mentioned an instruction manual of any sort until his fourth incarnation, when his companion Romana dug it out. Perhaps he'd procured it during his recent return to Gallifrey during the Vardan and Sontaran invasions... In any event, he claimed never to have used it. Romana, however, pointed out that it advised using both the synchronic feedback and the multi-loop stabiliser: 'On any capsule, it will be found impossible to effect a smooth materialisation without first activating the multi-loop stabiliser.' The Doctor dismissed this as absolute rubbish, though he was – by the end of their adventure on the pirate planet Zanak – using both devices.

THE PIRATE PLANET
by Douglas Adams
Starring Tom Baker as the Doctor
First broadcast:
30/09/1978–21/10/1978

INT. TARDIS

                THE DOCTOR
What are you reading?

                ROMANA
Oh, just familiarising myself with the technical details of this capsule.

                THE DOCTOR
Capsule? What kind of a word is that? If you mean TARDIS, why don't you say TARDIS?

                ROMANA
The Type 40 capsule wasn't on the main syllabus, you see.

                THE DOCTOR
Yes, I don't know what the Academy's coming to these days.

                ROMANA
Veteran and vintage vehicles was an optional extra.

THE PIRATE PLANET
by Douglas Adams

VENGEANCE ON VAROS
by Philip Martin
Starring Colin Baker as the Doctor
First broadcast:
19/01/1985–26/01/1985

The Doctor maintained his aversion to doing things by the book. Having briefly referred to it while undertaking some ill-advised repairs, not far from the planet Skonnos, he seems not to have consulted the manual again for many years. In fact, when the Sixth Doctor's companion Peri found it, it was propping open a vent. (The Doctor commented that he'd started reading it once.)

YOU CAN'T FLY THE TARDIS WITHOUT THE DOCTOR...

... unless you happen to be:
» The Time Lords,
remote-operating it
» The Master, stealing
or sabotaging it
» Romanadvoratrelundar,
doing it by the book
» Adric, doing it by accident
» Tegan, trusting
the Index File
» Tegan, not trusting
the Doctor
» Professor Hayter, as part
of the Xeraphin Gestalt
» Nyssa programming
a fast return
» Turlough, doing it
for the Black Guardian
» Kamelion, doing it
for the Master
» Grace Holloway, placing
it in a temporal orbit
» Rose, filled with Vortex energy
» Donna, filling the
Doctor with confidence
» The Children of Time,
guiding the Earth back home
» Gadget, being guided
back to Bowie Base One

Index File

As the Fourth Doctor gave way to the Fifth, his companions Nyssa and Tegan found themselves effectively in charge of the TARDIS as it plunged towards Event One – the Big Bang. They accessed the Index File of the TARDIS Information System, displayed on the monitor screen on the console, and Tegan followed on-screen instructions to take the TARDIS to Castrovalva. The Doctor later revealed that no such instructions existed – their flight had been pre-programmed by the Master as part of an elaborate trap for the Doctor.

TIME TRAVELS

When the TARDIS dematerialises from one physical or temporal location then rematerialises in another, it does not actually travel through any physical space. Instead, it spends the intervening time period travelling through the Time Vortex. Under the normal laws of physics understood by the likes of Einstein, energy is equal to mass multiplied by the speed of light squared ($E = MC^2$). Such laws do not apply in the Vortex; in its extra-temporal physics, energy is equal to mass multiplied by the speed of light cubed ($E = MC^3$). To those travelling within it, perception of the Vortex changes according to the travellers' own relation to their points of departure and destination. The effect of which is that the Vortex seems seems blue when travelling back in time and red when travelling into the future. The Doctor was once forced by the Axons to reveal the enormous power requirements of travel in the Time Vortex:

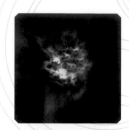

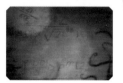

THE TIME TUNNEL

The first episode of *Doctor Who* in 1963 effectively established the principle that the show's opening titles depict travel through the Time Vortex, though the script made no reference to the Vortex itself, and the design has changed many times over the years.

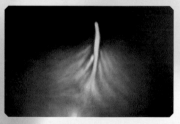

Temporal Hazards

Vortex travel is dangerous and difficult in itself, which is one reason why the Doctor and his companions often experience such a bumpy ride. Travelling back in time – against the natural forward progression of the fourth dimension – is particularly tricky. This, perhaps, is why the TARDIS still misses its destination sometimes, as when Rose visited Cardiff in 1869 (not Naples in 1860) with the Ninth Doctor and Queen Victoria in 1879 (not Ian Dury in 1979) with the Tenth.

It's a rare event, but the TARDIS has occasionally been caught up in a variety of temporal distortions, collisions and near misses. And, of course, it is not the only time machine out there...

》 The Daleks sent their own prototype time machine in pursuit of the First Doctor.

》 The Fourth Doctor was unable to land on Callufrax because the hollowed-out planet Zanak was attempting to materialise around it at the same moment.

》 Meglos, the last Zolfa-Thuran, trapped the Fourth Doctor and Romana in a chronic hysteris; they broke through by repeating their time-looped actions ahead of sequence.

》 The TARDIS was buffeted by turbulence from a stolen Concorde travelling down a Time Contour into Earth's prehistory.

》 Drifting into a warp ellipse, the TARDIS almost collided with Mawdryn's spaceship, which was travelling in the ellipse in a fixed temporal and spatial orbit.

》 A Dalek time corridor ensnared the TARDIS and dragged it to Earth in 1984.

》 The collision of time particles with a multidimensional implosion field caused an adverse Kontron effect when the TARDIS entered a Kontron tunnel.

TIME CRASH

What would happen if two TARDISes occupied precisely the same space-time coordinates?

Time Ram

If the atoms of one TARDIS inhabited the atoms of the other, the result would be the instant extinction of both. The Third Doctor threatened to time ram the Master's TARDIS rather than allow the Master to free a Chronovore. The Master called his bluff, but the Doctor's companion Jo actually initiated this time ram herself. The two TARDISes and their occupants were only saved from total destruction by the Chronovore itself.

THE TIME MONSTER
by Robert Sloman
Starring Jon Pertwee as the Doctor
First broadcast: 20/05/1972–24/06/1972

Gravity Bubble

Knowing that the TARDIS was about to materialise around a genuine police box, the Master got there first, and the Doctor's TARDIS ended up materialising around the Master's. This created a gravity bubble: entering the police box in the control room

took the Fourth Doctor and Adric into another, darker control room with a police box standing in it. Entering that box took them into a third control room, with yet another police box, and so on. This dimensionally recursive loop was not infinite, and the Doctor eventually ended up back outside his own TARDIS, in a lay-by at the side of a busy road. To generate enough power to break the TARDIS out of the gravity bubble, the Doctor had to jettison part of the ship's internal configuration (see page 95).

Temporal Collision

While its defences were down for repairs, the Tenth Doctor's TARDIS collided with the Fifth's, and the two time machines merged. The resulting paradox

TIME CRASH
by Steven Moffat
Starring David Tennant and Peter Davison as the Doctor
First broadcast: 16/11/2007

threatened to blow a hole in the space-time continuum the size of Belgium, which would trigger the end of the universe.

SPACE TRAVELS

The TARDIS can also operate like a more conventional spacecraft. It first materialises in space before continuing its journey, and is then prey to the same external forces that might threaten other space travellers...

>> The Animus dragged the ship down to the planet Vortis.

>> It suffered a bumpy Moon-landing in 2070 thanks to the effects of a Gravitron.

>> When its landing mechanism jammed, the TARDIS was stuck in the path of a Cyber missile.

>> There was a near-miss with an Earth cargo freighter in the 26th century.

>> The City on Exxilon drained the ship's power, stranding the Third Doctor and Sarah Jane with some marooned humans and Daleks.

>> Immobilised for repairs, the TARDIS collided with a Skonnon ship.

>> It passed through a Charged Vacuum Emboitment into the smaller universe of E-Space.

>> It was vulnerable to Earth defence satellite Sentinel Six in 2084.

>> It broke up under gravitational assault by the Tractators.

>> A Dalek signal dragged the TARDIS off-course to a landing in Utah, 2012.

>> Its defences down for repairs, the TARDIS impacted with the Sto cruiser *Titanic*.

SAVING THE DAY

Some Doctors have regarded the TARDIS as home, some Doctors have simply used It as transport. And, from time to time, the TARDIS itself has been vital to resolving a dangerous situation:

>> The Fourth Doctor used the TARDIS tractor beam to pull a neutron star off course and save the planet Chloris.

>> The Fifth Doctor materialised the TARDIS at the Master's landing coordinates, thus sending the Master back into the space-time continuum.

>> When a satellite struck a Navarino tourist space-bus, the Seventh Doctor generated an anti-gravity loop from his TARDIS and got the bus down to Earth.

>> Grace Holloway initiated a temporal orbit, allowing the TARDIS to reverse time and save Earth from being pulled inside out.

>> Blon Fel Fotch Pasameer-Day Slitheen looked into the heart of the TARDIS. The Time Vortex reverted her to an egg.

>> Rose Tyler, too, looked into the heart of the Time Vortex. Its energies poured into her, enabling her to destroy the Daleks.

>> The Tenth Doctor and his companions piloted the TARDIS from the Medusa Cascade, towing the Earth back to its solar system.

Unexpected Company...

The Doctor has invited many people on board the TARDIS over the centuries. He's also found a fair few stowaways, intruders and hitchhikers, among them:

>> Steven Taylor
>> Bret Vyon
>> Dodo Chaplet
>> Zoe Heriot
>> Sarah Jane Smith
>> Romanadvoratrelundar
>> Adric
>> Tegan Jovanka
>> Vislor Turlough
>> Vena, a Karfelan
>> H.G. Wells
>> Jackie Tyler
>> Donna Noble

... and Uninvited Guests

Theoretically, the TARDIS is indestructible and impregnable. It's never actually been destroyed, and most enemies have been repelled. But some beings, not always unfriendly, have been powerful (or lucky) enough to breach its defences, including:

>> The Celestial Toymaker
>> The Master of the
Land of Fiction
>> The Time Lords
>> Kronos, a Chronovore
>> Sutekh, an Osiran
>> The Mandragora Helix
>> The Nucleus of the Swarm
>> Sontaran troopers
>> The White Guardian
>> Biroc, a Tharil
>> The Keeper of Traken
>> Cybermen >> Omega
>> The Black Guardian
>> The Malus >> Tractators
>> A Segonax junk-mail satellite
>> The Master
>> A Dalek

TEMPORAL POWERS

The Doctor has encountered a number of races with some degree of time-travel ability or even control over time. While the Daleks have long rivalled the Time Lords as a temporal power, neither the Sontarans nor the Cybermen had any real time-travel abilities of their own. The Sontarans have been known to use Osmic Projection and stole a prototype time-travel device, modelled on Time Lord technology, from Space Station Chimera in the Third Zone. The Cybermen captured a time vessel that landed on the planet Telos, and planned to avert the destruction of their home planet, Mondas, in 1986. The Time Lords banned the Miniscope, which resembled their own time-scoop technology. The Osirans, like the Daleks, had time-corridor technology, and the Borad on the planet Karfel developed something similar. The long-extinct Jagaroth used warp engines, and the explosion of their last spaceship fragmented Scaroth, the last of his race, throughout Earth history. Humans also adopted warp-drive propulsion in space travel, and – with sufficient power – this could be used to punch time windows across great temporal and spatial distances. The now-defunct Time Agency issued its agents, like Captain Jack Harkness, with wrist-worn Vortex Manipulators, the space hopper of time travel. The time-sensitive Tharils were enslaved by humans and used as navigators in ships that rode the Time Winds. The ancient entity Fenric stirred up time storms to transport individuals through time and space in an instant. And then there are the Weeping Angels...

FX: The FULL ANGEL is now in the room standing in front of the screen! It's still a grainy, liney, video image (like Chris in Parting of the Ways or David in Blink) but its fangs are bared and one claw is reaching out for Amy. (Throughout this, the loop is still going, so the Video Angel breaks into mush for a tiny blip every three seconds.)

                    AMY
          Doctor!!

     CUT TO: EXT. ENCAMPMENT – NIGHT
     THE DOCTOR and RIVER.

                  RIVER SONG
          What does that mean? An
          image of a Weeping Angel
          is a Weeping Angel?

     The Doctor's face: mounting
     realisation.

THE TIME OF ANGELS
by Steven Moffat

JOURNEY LOG
The Time of Angels

Some time in the 171st century the Doctor and Amy are visiting the biggest museum ever when the Doctor spots a Home Box with an inscription in Old High Gallifreyan.

It's a message from River Song, calling him back to the 51st century, where he rescues her from the *Byzantium*, a galaxy-class category 4 starliner. When the ship crashes, there is a single survivor on board: a Weeping Angel.

THE TIME OF
ANGELS and
FLESH AND STONE
by Steven Moffat
Starring Matt Smith
as the Doctor
First broadcast:
24/04/2010–01/05/2010

The Doctor, Amy, River and an army of clerics discover more Weeping Angels at the site of the crash. Long stranded and deprived of anything to feed off, these Angels have been slowly dying and losing their forms; this is the beginning of their revival. They begin to prey on the humans among them, but not by transporting them back in time. Instead, their victims' necks are broken – the Angels are now feeding directly.

And they are revelling in the carnage...

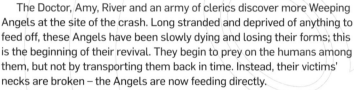

Don't Blink

The Tenth Doctor encountered four Weeping Angels in an abandoned house called Wester Drumlins in London in 2007. There a single touch from one transported him and Martha Jones back in time to the year 1969. Between 2005 and 2007, Wester Drumlins had been the scene of a series of disappearances, which a girl called Sally Sparrow learned were down to the Angels – the only race to kill people nicely. Their prey were zapped back in time and left to live to death, while

BLINK
by Steven Moffat
Starring David Tennant
as the Doctor
First broadcast:
09/06/2007

the Angels fed off the potential energy of the lives their victims would otherwise have led.

The Weeping Angels were quantum-locked – they were able to move only when they were unobserved. So the only defence against them was not to blink.

River Song

River Song is a younger version of the professor the Tenth Doctor met at The Library, who sacrificed herself to save him and over 4,000 people from the Vashta Nerada. He never learnt who she was, though she'd clearly met him in his own future and seemed closer to him than anybody ever had been: she even knew his real name. She also kept a diary describing adventures they were yet to have, and this younger River has the same battered blue notebook. The Doctor can apparently look forward to the Bone Meadows, a picnic at Asgard, and trips to the end of the universe and the singing towers at Darillium. According to Father Octavian, leader of a squad of Church troopers, River was until recently a prisoner at Stormcage Containment Facility, convicted of murder. She killed a good man – a hero to many...

📺 **SILENCE IN THE LIBRARY and FOREST OF THE DEAD**
by **Steven Moffat**
Starring David Tennant as the Doctor
First broadcast: 31/05/2008–07/06/2008

The Crooked Smile

There is a crack in a wall on the *Byzantium*'s Secondary Flight Deck, and it is the same shape as the crack in Amy's bedroom wall, as the crack in the hull of Starship UK, and as the crack in the War Room wall during the Blitz. The same crooked smile. The Doctor realises that time energy is spilling out of the crack. It erases every moment of the existence of anyone it comes into contact with so that they have never lived at all. The Angels call it the Time Field and predict that it will destroy reality.

The Doctor determines that the explosion that caused it is still happening, somewhere in time, and traces it to a specific date: 26 June 2010. The date of Amy Pond's wedding to Rory Williams.

HOW BIG IS BIG?

'J ust how big is the TARDIS?' Sarah Jane Smith once asked the Fourth Doctor. 'How big is big?' was his helpful response. 'There are no measurements in infinity.'

The TARDIS interior is infinitely flexible and dazzlingly vast, if not actually infinite. At one time, the ship had a measurable weight of 5 times 10 to the 6th kilos in an Earth-type gravity, or about 5,000 tonnes, (or 500 red London double-decker buses) and the Doctor has sometimes identified and isolated proportions of the internal architecture. But it seems to have infinite potential: its interior expands and reduces to suit the Doctor's needs at any given time. Its pedestrian infrastructure (or corridors, as humans would describe them) can seem endless, and even the Doctor has been known to get lost.

This is not helped by the fact that this infrastructure is unstable, so rooms and corridors actually rearrange themselves, seemingly at will.

This was probably yet another fault in the Doctor's borrowed TARDIS, which was in for repairs on Gallifrey when the First Doctor made off with it. But, like the broken Chameleon Circuit, it's a fault that he's grown to love. Indeed, it's likely that the TARDIS rearranges its own

contents, almost like a series of interlocking cogs, to suit the Doctor's needs at any given moment. After his recent regeneration, the Doctor had to contend with the contents of a swimming pool turning up in the library during the upheaval. But he was still delighted with the end result of the TARDIS's own regeneration.

There is also, of course, the facility for the Doctor to alter and adapt the architectural configuration of the TARDIS interior manually. As well as the various standard options for the control room decor – white-with-roundels, wood-panelled, Gothic, coral, leopard-skin – the rooms and corridors beyond the interior door have taken on an assortment of appearances of their own. The default for most internal areas seems to be to follow the current control room design, but this is by no means a hard-and-fast rule. The corridors stretching through the ship shared the original control room's roundelled look for a long time, but have also been brick-lined, stone-built, or ivy-strewn. Which probably raises the question of a fault in the TARDIS systems again.

These corridors, of course, link the TARDIS's eccentric arrangement of rooms with each other. The selection is intriguing, and is unlikely to be standard for a Gallifreyan time-travel capsule. This is a TARDIS whose owner has added and altered its interior dimensions, the rooms and their contents as the mood has taken him over the course of 900 years, aided and abetted by the TARDIS itself...

Jettisoning rooms

As part of the Architectural Configuration facility available to the Doctor, it is possible to jettison portions of the TARDIS interior in order to generate extra energy and momentum, or simply to tidy up by deleting unused rooms. He has done this at least three times:

Trapped in a gravity bubble (see page 86), extra power was needed

to free the TARDIS. The Fourth Doctor decided to jettison the bedroom recently vacated by his companion Romana.

Locked on a collision course with the hydrogen in-rush at the beginning of the universe, the Fifth Doctor calculated the extra energy requirements as 17,000 tons of thrust. He jettisoned a whole quarter of the TARDIS to provide this, unfortunately discarding the Zero Room in the process (see page 103).

The Seventh Doctor jettisoned the swimming pool (see page 99) having discovered that it was leaking.

Bedrooms

The TARDIS left Gallifrey equipped with beds that folded down out of the wall in the sleeping quarters adjacent to the control room and were shaped and curved to fit the humanoid form. When their first human companions Ian and Barbara joined the TARDIS, they shared a large dormitory area with the Doctor and his granddaughter Susan. After Susan's departure, new companion Vicki inherited her bed.

📺 **THE WEB PLANET**
by Bill Strutton
Starring William Hartnell as the Doctor
First broadcast:
13/02/1965–
20/03/1965

The Third Doctor may have scrapped these sleeping areas: at one stage there was a fold-down bed in a control-room wall. But by the end of the Fourth Doctor's time, his companions had more conventional bedrooms – first Romana, then Adric had rooms of their own, both using them to store and display various reminders of previous misadventures. Romana's room was jettisoned soon after

she stayed behind in E-Space; not long after his death, Adric's was taken by Turlough. Nyssa and Tegan shared a room,

📺 **THE VISITATION**
by Eric Saward
Starring Peter Davison as the Doctor
First broadcast:
15/02/1982–
23/02/1982

where Nyssa conducted small scientific experiments and once constructed a sonic booster to fight off a Terileptil android.

Laboratory

The Second Doctor, Jamie and Victoria analysed a sample of a weed creature here, discovering that it was emitting a toxic gas. A microscope revealed 'little wriggly things' in the sample, and the Doctor concluded that the seaweed was as alive as any human being.

Power Room

After using an emergency unit to take the TARDIS out of time and space to escape an encroaching lava flow, the Second Doctor made repairs in the Power Room.

Wardrobe Room

In the Ninth and Tenth Doctor's TARDIS, the Wardrobe Room was reached by taking the first left out of the control room, then second right, third on the left, straight ahead, under the stairs, past the bins, the fifth door on the left. (Earlier TARDIS configurations had tended to keep it a little closer to the control room.) It contained a comprehensive selection of garments from planets across the universe, supplemented by items obtained by the Doctor in his travels or left by his companions. Many of the Doctor's companions selected outfits from its racks, as did the Doctor. These included:

》 An Ulster cape the First Doctor had acquired from Gilbert and Sullivan **》** Full Viking dress, complete with horned helmet, a King of Hearts outfit, and a Pierrot costume – the Fourth Doctor's first three outfit choices **》** The Fourth Doctor's final choice of outfit: wide-brimmed hat, jacket and trousers, and a long multicoloured scarf knitted for him by Madame Nostradamus **》** Victoria Waterfield's dress, which Sarah Jane Smith found and wore on a visit to England in 1911 **》** An outfit for a noblewoman of Tara, worn by Romana **》** The Sixth Doctor's garish assemblage, and a glittering bright blue jacket selected by Lt. Hugo Lang **》** One of Napoleon's uniforms, a bearskin hat, a mortarboard and hat, a long scarf, coat and hat, a velvet smoking jacket and frilly shirt, cricket whites, and an enormous fur coat – all rejected by the Seventh Doctor **》** The Seventh Doctor's eventual selection: checked trousers, question-mark pullover, cream jacket and battered panama hat **》** Rose Tyler's Victorian-era dress **》** The shoes, suit, tie and coat chosen by the Tenth Doctor after his regeneration

BUILDING A WARDROBE

Russell T Davies's script for *The Christmas Invasion* included a scene featuring the new Doctor choosing his clothes, and the production team leapt at the first chance since *Doctor Who*'s revival to create a new room in the TARDIS. The scene was filmed on part of the standing control-room set, redressed by the Art Department with several racks of clothing. Most of the clothes were contributed by the Costume Department, but Producer Phil Collinson brought in a long scarf – à la Tom Baker's Doctor – which had been knitted for him when he was a child. Phil was hoping the scarf might be visible among all the different outfits, but it actually ended up draped round David Tennant's neck for one brief scene.

When the final edit of the episode was completed, digital effects house The Mill enhanced and extended the new Wardrobe Room, adding in computer-generated imagery of many more racks of clothes and a helical staircase leading back up to the control room.

Boot Cupboard

An enormous salon containing a pair of boots, discovered by Sarah Jane Smith. She thought it was a bit big for a boot cupboard; the Doctor said he'd seen bigger boot cupboards.

Cricket Club

Rediscovered by the Fifth Doctor soon after his regeneration, this was full of cricketing trophies.

Tool Room

Where the Seventh Doctor kept his Radiation Wave Meter.

Bathroom

A large recreational area adorned with reclining chairs, occasional tables (with a copy of the *Daily Mirror* reporting on the sinking of the *Titanic*), statues, trees and large potted plants. It also contained a swimming pool, at least until a leak prompted the Seventh Doctor to jettison it. The pool was later replaced, but its contents ended up in the Library, where the newly regenerated Doctor got soaked as the TARDIS crash-landed in Amelia Pond's back garden.

Ancillary Power Station

The Sontaran invasion of Gallifrey forced the Doctor and a few friends to retreat inside the TARDIS. The alien troops breached the ship, however, and pursued the Doctor's party through the time machine. Their goal was the Ancillary Power Station, which housed the TARDIS's back-up generator. The Doctor had disguised the Power Station as an art gallery, in which were hung several famous paintings, including:

》》 *The Arnolfini Portrait* by Jan van Eyck (1434) 》》 *The Fighting Temeraire, Tugged to Her Last Berth to be Broken Up*, 1838 by J.M.W. Turner (1839) 》》 *The Snail* by Henri Matisse (1953)

Pressing a concealed button near the base of the statue of Aphrodite of Melos (known as Venus de Milo) that stood in front of the Matisse removed the illusion – the artworks faded away to leave an empty room. On the bare brick walls was the control for the ancillary power generator.

Greenhouse

Full of examples of alien flora. A Sontaran trooper was briefly trapped inside one of these plants.

STRIKING SETS

In the 1970s, industrial action at the BBC was a regular part of the calendar: many programmes were affected by strikes by scene-shifters, electricians, lighting technicians and so on. In 1979, industrial action ended production on *Shada*, the six-part finale to *Doctor Who*'s seventeenth season. Despite the completion of its location filming and a large proportion of its studio work, the story had to be dropped from the schedules.

Two years before *Shada* was abandoned, threatened strike action almost forced the cancellation of *The Invasion of Time*, the climax to Season 15. With studio space allocated to other shows, Producer

Graham Williams decided to take advantage of the situation and set a larger than normal number of scenes inside the TARDIS and to explore further inside the time machine than had ever been done before. These interior scenes were filmed on location at a disused hospital in Surrey, which gave the TARDIS corridors and several of its new rooms a uniquely bricks-and-mortar appearance. The control room set was also assembled at this location, giving its sound an echo unique to this story.

Sickbay
An area of the TARDIS where the Doctor and friends hid from the Sontarans.

Workshop
The Time Lady Rodan built a Demat Gun, under hypnosis and K-9's supervision, in the TARDIS workshop. The Doctor used the weapon to end the Sontaran invasion.

Cloisters

Adric once discovered the Fourth
Doctor glumly pondering the nature
of entropy while wandering these
covered walkways deep inside the
TARDIS. They were a continuation
of the usual white-walled corridors

with their continuous pattern of roundels, but there were also wooden
benches and stone pillars which were overgrown with trailing ivy – a sign,
the Doctor muttered, of how the TARDIS was ageing and decaying in
accordance with the laws of Thermodynamics. He told Adric not to disturb
him if he was pacing up and down in this part of the TARDIS, unless it was
terribly urgent, in which case he could ring the Cloister Bell.

Tegan Jovanka later got lost in the cloisters, and the Master briefly hid
his TARDIS there.

The Cloister Room

The cloisters led to the Cloister Room, containing the TARDIS's link to
the Eye of Harmony, the heart of the ship's power until the destruction
of Gallifrey (see page 8). In the Eighth Doctor's TARDIS, this was a huge
Gothic chamber, entered through a pair of massive doors that flew open
at the touch of a human. The floor was covered with dried-up leaves, large

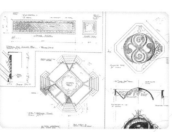

stone staircases led to balconies and other levels, and there were bats in the ceiling. At the centre of the room, at the top of a ramp, was the Eye itself. This was a crypt-like structure resembling a gigantic closed eye. Tall pillars stood at its corners; removing one allowed a human to gaze into a shaft of light and open the Eye. The Eighth Doctor's battle with the Master climaxed here.

Library

An area to one side of the large control room used by the Seventh and Eighth Doctors, its shelves lined with leather-bound tomes and paperback copies of works like *The Time Machine* by H.G. Wells. Nearby filing cabinets held bags of gold dust, and there was a Louis XV chair next to a standard lamp and a pair of occasional tables, on one of which stood a glass bowl of jelly babies. A few paces from the armchair was an antique gramophone and a collection of shellac records that included Pat Hodge singing 'In A Dream'.

The Zero Room

This was situated on one of the lower levels of the TARDIS, close to the ship's main drives and a long way from the control room. Two plain white doors opened onto a wide, pale-walled and empty space. This room, the Fifth Doctor told his companions, cancelled out all external influences and distractions – it was entirely cut off from the rest of the universe. Its walls and doors were made of a material that generated stabilising effects.

The purpose of the Zero Room was to provide a neutral environment conducive to mental and physical healing. It was a standard feature of the Time Lords' time-travel capsules and, like similar rooms on Gallifrey, was a place where Time Lords could recuperate in the aftermath of bodily regeneration. After the trauma of his regeneration from his fourth body, this was just what the Doctor needed. He was able to enter a trance-like state, levitating a little way off the floor, and begin to mend his damaged synapses.

Unfortunately, when the Doctor had to delete rooms to generate enough thrust to escape Event One, he was unable to specify which parts of the TARDIS could be destroyed. Returning to the Zero Room, he discovered that it had been part of the twenty-five per cent that had been

jettisoned. Only the doors remained, and Nyssa used them to construct an improvised 'Zero Cabinet', hoping to replicate the effects of the Zero Room until they could find a similar area of absolute simplicity where the Doctor could complete his convalescence.

Regeneration

A process of bodily renewal, whereby every cell in a Time Lord's body is replaced and he becomes, to all intents and purposes, a completely new man. The regeneration cycle lasts fifteen hours, and can be initiated by old age, near-fatal injury or illness, or simply at will. It effects a comprehensive change in physical appearance, and can result in significant differences in personality.

At some point in Gallifreyan history, the Time Lords seem to have established a limit of twelve regenerations, or thirteen lives, after

which the body began to decay. This was perhaps connected to Rassilon's desire to prevent any of his presidential successors gaining immortality and ruling for ever. It is, however, known that it was perfectly possible for the High Council to grant a complete new life cycle: they offered one to the Master as a reward for entering the Death Zone and rescuing the first five Doctors; much later, the Master was actually resurrected to fight for Gallifrey in the Time War, complete with the ability to regenerate.

THE DOCTOR'S REGENERATIONS

Thanks to an adventurous lifestyle, the Doctor has run through his lives at a much faster rate than most Time Lords did...

Regeneration: First

The First Doctor had already lived a long life by the time he left Gallifrey with his granddaughter, and he was probably even older than he looked. He had the appearance of an elderly man, and suffered from the aches and pains of old age, often complaining that his legs were not as young as they used to be. Eventually, his body wore thin, and he underwent his first regeneration.

THE TENTH PLANET
by Kit Pedler & Gerry Davis
Starring William Hartnell as the Doctor
First broadcast: 08/10/1966–29/10/1966

THE POWER OF THE DALEKS
by David Whitaker
Starring Patrick Troughton as the Doctor
First broadcast: 05/11/1966–10/12/1966

» Last words: 'Ah, yes! Thank you. It's good. Keep warm.'

» First words: 'Slower... Slower... Concentrate on one thing. One thing!' Having reached the TARDIS, the old Doctor collapsed to the floor. As the time machine's controls began to operate themselves and the ship dematerialised, the Doctor's companions Ben and Polly stood back and watched as a white glow enveloped his features, then cleared to reveal a new, younger man. He was a little shorter, with untidy dark hair surrounding an unfamiliar face, and even his clothes seemed to have changed. The stranger's explanations were cryptic at best, but he did mutter something about 'renewal', adding: 'It's part of the TARDIS. Without it, I couldn't survive.'

Regeneration: Second

It is not known where the Doctor's second change took place. The TARDIS deposited his unconscious third form on Earth in the midst of the arrival of a Nestene spearhead. The regeneration itself was ordered by a Time Lord tribunal, which had found him guilty of meddling in the affairs of other civilisations. The Doctor's punishment was a period of exile on 20th-century Earth, and a change of appearance. He was allowed to choose his new face, but made such a fuss about the selection on offer that the Time Lords lost patience and took the decision for him.

THE WAR GAMES
by Terrance Dicks & Malcolm Hulke
Starring Patrick Troughton as the Doctor
First broadcast: 19/04/1969–21/06/1969

SPEARHEAD FROM SPACE
by Robert Holmes
Starring Jon Pertwee as the Doctor
First broadcast: 03/01/1970–24/01/1970

» Last words: 'No! Stop! You're making me giddy! No, you can't do this to me! No! No! No! No! No! No!' **»** First words:'Shoes... Must find my shoes.'

Regeneration: Third

The Doctor's third regeneration was caused by the damage inflicted on his body by radiation from the blue crystals of Metebelis Three. The Doctor had watched as the ruler of the Giant Spiders was destroyed. He then collapsed into the TARDIS and allowed the ship to take him home. 'Home', after his long exile, was Earth and UNIT HQ. The damage to his body was so severe that the Doctor was unable to regenerate until another Time Lord kick-started the process. Even then, it took the new Doctor much longer than previously to recover from his regeneration, and he spent a long period unconscious in the UNIT sickbay.

PLANET OF THE SPIDERS
by Robert Sloman
Starring Jon Pertwee as the Doctor
First broadcast: 04/05/1974–08/06/1974

ROBOT
by Terrance Dicks
Starring Tom Baker as the Doctor
First broadcast: 28/12/1974–18/01/1975

» Last words: 'A tear, Sarah Jane? No, don't cry. While there's life, there's...' **»** First words: '... typical Sontaran attitude... stop Linx... perverting the course of human history...'

Regeneration: Fourth

Having saved the universe from the Master, the Fourth Doctor fell to his death from the top of a radio telescope on Earth. At first haunted by images

of his enemies demanding his death, he then saw visions of each of his companions. The Doctor had known that the end was near, as he had been constantly haunted by a ghostly figure known as the Watcher – a projection of the Doctor's next life. The wraith and the Doctor became one, leaving a new, much younger Doctor in

📺 **LOGOPOLIS**
by Christopher H. Bidmead
Starring Tom Baker and Peter Davison as the Doctor
First broadcast:
28/02/1981–21/03/1981

📺 **CASTROVALVA**
by Christopher H. Bidmead
Starring Peter Davison as the Doctor
First broadcast:
04/01/1982–12/01/1982

their place. The new Doctor suffered more post-regenerative ill-effects than he ever had before. His damaged nervous system required the tranquillity of the Zero Room to recover (see page 103).

▶▶ Last words: 'It's the end, but the moment has been prepared for.' ▶▶ First words: 'I... Oh.'

Regeneration: Fifth

The Fifth Doctor sacrificed his life to save his companion Peri – both were infected with Spectrox Toxaemia, but there was enough antidote for

📺 **THE CAVES OF ANDROZANI**
by Robert Holmes
Starring Peter Davison and Colin Baker as the Doctor
First broadcast:
08/03/1984–16/03/1984

📺 **THE TWIN DILEMMA**
by Anthony Steven
Starring Colin Baker as the Doctor
First broadcast:
22/03/1984–30/03/1984

only one of them. The faces of his friends seemed to appear in front of him, encouraging him to go on; but the Master's image also appeared, insisting that it was time for the Doctor to die. The Doctor's post-regenerative behaviour was its most erratic yet, and he even attempted to strangle Peri. But regenerating inside the TARDIS may have helped, since the Sixth

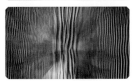

Doctor's abrasively self-confident character was already asserting itself.

▶▶ Last words: 'Going soon. It's time to say goodbye. Might regenerate, I don't know. Feels different this time. Adric?' ▶▶ First words: 'You were expecting someone else?'

Regeneration: Sixth

The change between the Sixth and Seventh Doctors occurred in the TARDIS control room, which may have helped it to be a little smoother than had often been the case in the past.

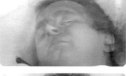

📺 **TIME AND THE RANI**
by Pip & Jane Baker
Starring Sylvester McCoy as the Doctor
First broadcast:
07/09/1987–28/09/1987

The new Doctor suffered some brief amnesia and had a tendency to use muddled aphorisms, but he recovered his memory quite quickly.

The regeneration itself was caused by an assault by another Time Lord, the Rani. She used energy beams to force the TARDIS into a crash-landing on the planet Lakertya.

The Rani then took advantage of the Doctor's confused post-regenerative state to convince him she was his companion, Mel.

➤➤ Last words: Unknown
➤➤ First words: 'Oh no, Mel. Ah, that was a nice nap. Now, down to business.'

Regeneration: Seventh

This was another traumatic change, with the Seventh Doctor shot as he left the TARDIS and then killed on a hospital operating table when a

📺 **DOCTOR WHO**
by Matthew Jacobs
Starring Paul McGann and Sylvester McCoy as the Doctor
First UK broadcast:
27/05/1996

well-meaning surgeon attempted to save his life, but was thrown by the Doctor's alien physiology. With Dr Holloway unable to operate on him, the Doctor's hearts went into arrest and he

died. It took several hours for the regeneration process to begin, with the result that the Eighth Doctor awoke miles from the TARDIS, suffering from severe amnesia and with no idea of who he was. He had no more than flashes of recent

memory until the Master opened the TARDIS's link to the Eye of Harmony, which somehow helped the new Doctor rediscover his identity.

➤➤ Last words: '... timing malfunction... the Master... He's out there... I've got to stop him.'
➤➤ First words: 'Who am I? Who am I?'

Regeneration: Eighth

There is no record of this regeneration, which may well have taken place during or immediately after the Time War. It is possible the new Doctor's meeting with Rose Tyler was soon after his regeneration.

Regeneration: Ninth

Rose Tyler saved the Doctor from extermination by absorbing power from the Time Vortex and turning it against the Daleks, but the power was lethal to her human form. The Doctor in turn saved Rose by drawing all the Vortex energy out of her and into himself, in the process harming his own body to such an extent that it precipitated his next regeneration. The Doctor stood upright in the TARDIS control room, as flames of regeneration energy erupted from him and his features

📺 **THE PARTING OF THE WAYS**
by Russell T Davies
Starring Christopher Eccleston and David Tennant as the Doctor
First broadcast: 18/06/2005

📺 **BORN AGAIN**
by Russell T Davies
Starring David Tennant as the Doctor
First broadcast: 18/11/2005

📺 **THE CHRISTMAS INVASION**
by Russell T Davies
Starring David Tennant as the Doctor
First broadcast: 25/12/2005

began to change...The Tenth Doctor seemed at first unaffected by the now-expected post-regenerative problems, but this did not last: the regeneration began to fail, and he spent much of the fifteen-hour regeneration cycle unconscious, until he was healed by a superheated infusion of free radicals and tannin (vapours from a cup of tea reacting with TARDIS machinery).

▶▶ Last words: 'Rose, before I go, I just want to tell you. You were fantastic. Absolutely fantastic. And d'you know what? So was I.'

▶▶ First words: 'Hello! Okay— Oh. New teeth. That's weird. So where was I? Oh, that's right. Barcelona.'

Regeneration: Tenth

The end came for the Tenth Doctor not at the hands of the Master, who came back from the dead to transplant himself into everyone on planet Earth. Nor was it inflicted by the Time Lords, who attempted to return from the timelocked Time War, intending to bring about the End of Time. It wasn't even caused by the injuries the Doctor sustained plunging down from a Vinvocci spaceship into the Naismith mansion, where he confronted the Master and Rassilon. The Tenth Doctor regenerated because he could not let one small, unimportant old man die. The Doctor sacrificed himself to save Wilfred Mott from a chamber flooded with radiation.

THE END OF TIME
by Russell T Davies
Starring David Tennant and Matt Smith as the Doctor
First broadcast: 25/12/2009-01/01/2010

As we've seen before with the Third Doctor, it takes Time Lords quite a while to die from radiation poisoning. The Doctor used this respite to get his reward, saying farewell to his friends and former companions. Just after seeing Rose Tyler one last time, he finally started to die as snow fell on the Powell Estate and the Ood sang him to his rest.

» Last words: 'I don't want to go.'
» First words: 'Legs! Still got legs, good!!'

INT. TARDIS - NIGHT

The song continues. THE DOCTOR at the console.

More pain. Fights it off. But it's time.

He stands back. Closer to the ramp. Ready, but never ready for this. Then, quietly:

                              THE DOCTOR
        I don't want to go.

And then, slowly...

FX: CU THE DOCTOR, as gently, a shroud of calm GOLDEN GLOW rises up around his head, his features still visible.

FX: MID-SHOT DOCTOR, lifting his GLOWING HANDS, in amazement, his face still visible within its glow.

And then, a sudden acceleration, wham - !

FX: THE DOCTOR VOLCANOES!!!! LONG SHOT, GOLDEN ENERGY blasting out of his head, his arms - beautiful, ferocious -

FX: GOLDEN ENERGY from one arm - ripping into the console - MASSIVE PRAC EXPLOSIONS, the whole thing going up - !

FX: GOLDEN ENERGY from the other arm, rips down the ramp - BLASTING THE DOORS, a MASSIVE SHEET OF FLAME flaring up!

PRAC FX: the door-windows shatter out!

FX: CRANING UP, WIDE SHOT, ENERGY still BLASTING OUT OF THE DOCTOR - PRAC FLAMES erupting all around, up through the floor! He's standing in the middle of an inferno!

The Cloister Bell tolling!

FX: CU the Doctor's head, GOLDEN ENERGY streaming out, his features finally disappearing... A new face forming...

FX: He snaps upright, ENERGY BURNING AWAY, fast, gone!

And there he is. Blinking. Dazed.

The New Man.

THE END OF TIME
by Russell T Davies

5

MATERIALISATION

The TARDIS doesn't – usually – fly. It disappears from one location and reappears in another. The ship's arrival is presaged by the noise of its engines, a distinctive wheezing and groaning sound that begins faintly, then increases in volume as the police-box shape starts to form, ending in a deep thud as the TARDIS solidifies. This arrival displaces the atoms occupying the space into which the TARDIS is introducing itself, so any onlooker feels a strong, churning wind that stirs up objects like fallen leaves and old newspapers in a small storm. Having landed ('materialised, I think, is the better word,' said the First Doctor), the TARDIS's occupants can then emerge safely through the external doors and become part of events on a new planet or in a new time period...

WHAT IS THAT NOISE?

The weird sound heard whenever the TARDIS lands actually dates all the way back to *Doctor Who*'s first ever episode. As William Hartnell flicked a few switches in late 1963, an unearthly abrasive roaring was heard – the work of Brian Hodgson of the BBC Radiophonic Workshop. This extraordinary noise was achieved by scraping a front-door key up and down a piano wire. The recorded result was then looped and played back at very slow speeds, with various hisses and beeps added to the mix. A dull thudding sound was added to the start of a take-off and to the end of a landing.

Strangely, the completed sound effect was actually registered as a piece of music. It was rarely heard in the programme in its entirety, and sometimes not at all: there were many instances of the TARDIS arriving or departing silently (or with a gentle hum) in those early years. Other sound effects were occasionally used during the 1960s, and it was ten years before Hodgson's effect became a standard part of every TARDIS journey. But when the series was revived in 2005, so was the sound effect, with added wind noises. From *Rose* onwards, it even formed the basis – in even slower playback – of the background sounds heard throughout scenes set inside the control room.

EFFECTING A DEMATERIALISATION

When we see the TARDIS arrive in a new location, we're watching a computer-generated effect added to the recorded footage by digital effects house The Mill. Back in 2004, The Mill devised a number of potential ways to show a materialisation, but the production team ultimately decided to replicate the gradual fading into existence that had characterised the TARDIS's arrival throughout the original run, and the same effect is still being used.

Production Designer Edward Thomas has always been keen to show the TARDIS's interaction with each new environment – the ship's arrival kicks up a storm, and wind machines are used to create a swirl of debris, or fluttering leaves or a flickering candle as the police box solidifies. The Mill contributed a particularly fine example of this

for *The Unquiet Dead* in 2005, with digitally created snowflakes settling on the TARDIS window ledges as it materialised, which then fell to the ground when it departed.

During the 1960s, 1970s and 1980s, such CGI wasn't even a dream for people working in television. At that time, the show's makers tried several ways of depicting a materialisation. One frequent method, especially in the very early years, was achieved during live recording in the studio by cross-fading between a photograph of a TARDIS-free set

and the set itself with the TARDIS in place. A later technique was to film the empty location then lock the camera in position; once the TARDIS prop or model had been put in place, camera recording resumed. The two pictures were mixed together during editing.

Routine Landing Procedures

Each Doctor has had his own idiosyncrasies when it comes to what to do immediately after a landing. The First Doctor was fastidious about taking readings for external conditions before venturing out of his ship: he would check gravity, air quality, soil composition, radiation levels, temperature and time period – at least so long as the TARDIS's instruments and gauges were functioning well enough to do so. The Second Doctor seemed less particular, but his superficially slapdash approach tended to be part of his act of misdirection; when challenged, he could reel off the details of external conditions without seeming to glance at the console. This trait was shared by several later incarnations, though the Third Doctor returned to the more conscientious approach of the First.

Checking the scanner for the view just outside the ship has generally been another regular part of the Doctor's safety checks, assuming that it's not been on the blink at the time. The scanner can display a rotating 360-degree view, though the Doctor has frequently been too impatient to wait and watch it through before making a dash for the doors...

Main Doors

Like the rest of the internal architecture, the doors leading out from the control room to wherever the TARDIS has landed have shifted and changed several times. The first seven Doctors all used a large set of double doors, in the same sterile white as the rest of the control room. For a long time, these seemed to lead directly outside, so it was possible to see the ship's surroundings through the open doors. Perhaps as part of the TARDIS's redecorations while the Third and Fourth Doctors were at the helm, some additional interface was eventually introduced – perhaps a short corridor bridging the interior and exterior dimensions and leading from the control-room doors to the police box doors. This meant that it was usually impossible to see outside the ship except via the scanner. The TARDIS architecture

has never, of course, been entirely stable, so this was not always the case: the Fourth Doctor once showed Sarah Jane Smith a view through the doorway of a future Earth ravaged by an unchecked Sutekh the Destroyer.

The much larger, darkened doorway from the Eighth Doctor's TARDIS may have restored the more direct threshold between the interior and the exterior. Dr Grace Holloway noted a sensation of spatial displacement as she accompanied the Doctor into the TARDIS and, moments before, a police

motorcyclist had ridden into the box – and, several moments later, he drove straight out again.

At some point during or after the dreadful events of the Time War, the battle-scarred TARDIS reconfigured its control room with a coral theme. As part of this, the direct link between the interior and exterior

📺 **PYRAMIDS OF MARS**
by Stephen Harris
Starring Tom Baker as the Doctor
First broadcast: 25/10/1975–15/11/1975

became permanent: the main doors now looked like the inner sides of the wooden doors of an actual police box, complete with a telephone cabinet on the right-hand door. Once again, there was a direct view through the open doors to whatever was outside. This seemingly unprotected and flimsy exit was protected by the ship's force field, now supplemented by power from a tribophysical waveform macro-kinetic extrapolator wired into the TARDIS defence systems. The Doctor was now able to open the doors during flight to show, say, Donna the birth of planet Earth, or rescue her from a Roboform-driven black cab.

THE RUNAWAY BRIDE
by Russell T Davies
Starring David Tennant
as the Doctor
First broadcast:
25/12/2006

PILOT

Doctor Who's first episode, *An Unearthly Child*, was actually recorded twice, after a first attempt was deemed unsatisfactory. Head of Drama Sydney Newman noted a number of problems with that pilot recording, not least being that the main doors failed to close properly once the cast had all entered the TARDIS control room. The large double doors had to be pulled shut by frantic stage hands.

The Eleventh Doctor's new TARDIS control room has kept this element of its previous appearance, with a set of police-box doors leading straight outside the ship. In fact, part of Amy's very first trip involved an unconventional new approach to seeing the wonders of space:

Some Unfortunate Landings

'We're falling!' 'Hold on! Hold on! Hold on!'

'Trust you to bring us down right in the middle of the sea.'

'We seem to be halfway up a mountain. We're balanced on the edge.'

'Not up to CAA standard, but a landing's a landing!'

'Are you quite sure this is the planet you aimed for?' 'Mm-mm. Fancy a swim?'

'Ah...'

'Are you okay?' 'Just had a fall.'

Materialise into Danger

The Doctor's granddaughter Susan once told Ian and Barbara that the point of materialisation is the most dangerous stage of any journey. Indeed, her grandfather panicked when the doors opened themselves just as the ship was materialising on 20th-century Earth, telling them that 'the space pressure was far too great.' He was right to be concerned: whatever external pressures are brought to bear as the TARDIS lands had, this time, compressed the time machine and the travellers to microscopic size. They found themselves stranded among gigantic insects and oversized matchboxes, unable to make themselves seen or heard.

📺 **PLANET OF GIANTS**
by Louis Marks
Starring William Hartnell as the Doctor
First broadcast:
31/10/1964–14/11/1964

📺 **THE ENEMY OF THE WORLD**
by David Whitaker
Starring Patrick Troughton as the Doctor
First broadcast:
23/12/1967–27/01/1968

The Second Doctor later discovered that it was equally dangerous for the TARDIS to dematerialise with its doors open. A future Earth dictator named Salamander, an exact double of the Doctor, tried to hijack the TARDIS, but took off without first closing the main doors. He was sucked out of the ship and into a void beyond, perhaps into the Time Vortex itself.

The exterior shell of the TARDIS is more or less indestructible and impregnable, but it does seem to be subject to external influences to some degree: external sounds can be heard inside the control room; an explosion outside can be felt by the ship's occupants; when the TARDIS landed at the South Pole, the sub-zero temperatures could be felt inside; on Spiridon, fungus spores covering the exterior doors deprived the interior of oxygen; the Tenth Doctor and Donna felt the impact of the removal of Earth from its solar system. It seems that the essentially inviolable state of the TARDIS interior is partially compromised by the physical link between its interior and exterior dimensions. One compensation though is that, having rematerialised in our dimension, it is able to fly.

>> The Second Doctor seems to have piloted the TARDIS from space to the Moon.

>> Archaeologists on Telos may have witnessed the TARDIS descending onto the planet surface.

>> The Fourth Doctor materialised the TARDIS above the Thames, intending to sink his ship in the river and open the doors to flush the Master out. Instead the TARDIS plummeted down onto the deck of a moored barge.

>> The TARDIS appeared in mid air over the Powell Estate, where the newly regenerated Tenth Doctor steered it to an extremely bumpy landing.

>> The Tenth Doctor flew the TARDIS along a busy motorway in pursuit of the Roboform-driven taxi that had kidnapped Donna Noble, later commenting that the TARDIS doesn't actually do much flying...

>> ... though he later showed off to Donna by flying the ship up into the night sky...

>> ... and to Wilfred Mott, when he flew the TARDIS over Chiswick so Donna could wave goodbye to her grandfather.

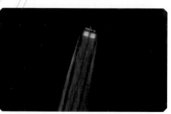

SAFETY MEASURES

There are three main elements to the TARDIS's post-materialisation safeguards:

▶▶ The Hostile Action Displacement System (HADS): If the TARDIS is attacked, it automatically dematerialises, before selecting a safer nearby location and reappearing. The Second Doctor had remembered to set the HADS when a Kroton tried

to disperse the TARDIS, but he never mentioned (or used) this function again, possibly because the ship selected a stupid place to land: halfway up a cliff.

▶▶ Pause Control: While it is not usually programmed to auto-operate, inserting the key in the lock after an interrupted journey could cancel the pause control and allow the TARDIS to continue on its original course. The Fourth Doctor probably deactivated this function

after it left him and Sarah Jane stranded on the planet Oseidon.

▶▶ Drift Compensators: These can be set to prevent the TARDIS slipping away from its coordinates, or programmed so that – if set adrift – the craft locks onto the nearest centre of gravity. When the Starship *Titanic* was holed by meteoroids, the TARDIS was among the debris pouring out into space; with the *Titanic* orbiting the Earth at the time of impact, the TARDIS headed for the planet below.

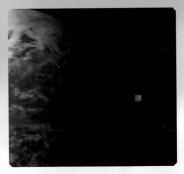

JOURNEY LOG
The Vampires of Venice

As they leave the site of the crashed *Byzantium*, Amy asks the Doctor to take her home. There she shows him her wedding dress, telling him she's supposed to be marrying Rory Williams on 26 June 2010. The Doctor immediately recognises the date – it's the source of the explosion in time that's caused the crooked-smile crack. He makes a quick detour to pick up Rory from his stag-do, then takes his two companions on a proper romantic date...

```
EXT. VENICE, 1580. STREET / CANAL - DAY 1

The ancient engines grind as the TARDIS materialises.

The Doctor and Amy and Rory step out into an explosion of
light and sound and colour.

Amy gasps. We spin around and take in the scene.

FX: DMP. We're in Venice, on the bank of the Grand Canal.
```

THE VAMPIRES OF VENICE
by Toby Whithouse

The Doctor pilots the TARDIS to Venice in 1580, planning to give Amy and Rory some time together. There they are told of something magical and evil going on at the House of Calvierri, whose young, pale-faced female occupants have fangs, don't like sunlight and can't be seen in mirrors. It's a classic case of vampire infestation (and no Time Lord likes a vampire).

📺 **THE VAMPIRES OF VENICE**
by Toby Whithouse
Starring Matt Smith as the Doctor
First broadcast: 08/05/2010

But the Sisters of the Water are no vampires. Rosanna Calvierri is the head of a family of sea-dwelling aliens who have fled the loss of their home world, Saturnyne. They

plan to save their race from extinction by turning Earth into a second Saturnyne. They have begun a slow process of repopulating the planet by draining the water from their human female recruits' bodies, then replacing it with alien blood. Meanwhile, 10,000 Saturnyne males are in the canals of Venice, waiting for their brides...

Perception Filter

The Sisters of the Water hide their true aquatic form using a perception filter – their appearance remains unchanged, but they manipulate the brainwaves of anyone looking at them so they see a humanoid disguise. The onlooker's subconscious is aware of the potential threat, however, and tries to warn the conscious brain, which is why the Sisters seem to have fangs.

The Chameleon Circuit of the TARDIS may incorporate some sort of sophisticated perception filter as part of the ship's own defences, and the Tenth Doctor once used TARDIS keys to rig up personal filters for himself, Martha Jones and Captain Jack Harkness, enabling them to move unseen around the world under the domination of the Master and the Toclafane. There was also a perception filter around the fob watch containing the Doctor's Time Lord essence after he'd used a Chameleon Arch to evade the Family of Blood.

The Crooked Smile

The crack in reality is somehow present everywhere the Doctor and Amy go, and now Rosanna Calvierri tells him that she fled Saturnyne when her home planet was crushed by the silence as a crack snapped shut behind it. River Song has already told the Doctor that he'll see her again when the Pandorica opens, something he quickly dismissed as a fairy tale. But he is now very aware that there is something very wrong in the universe, and it's somehow connected to – and perhaps even centred on – Amy Pond...

MORE THAN
A MACHINE?

'**M**y machine can't think,' the First Doctor once told his companions. He understood the technicalities; he knew that the ship's power was somehow contained beneath the column at the heart of the console; but at that time he had still to comprehend the true nature of that power. Ironically, the TARDIS was at that very moment doing its best to alert him that it was on the brink of disaster. Plunging back through time towards the beginning of the universe, thanks to a jammed switch, the TARDIS had tried to give him a series of clues – melted clock faces, repeated images of part journeys on the scanner screen, electric shocks from certain console controls.

📺 **THE EDGE OF DESTRUCTION**
by David Whitaker
Starring William Hartnell as the Doctor
First broadcast:
08/02/1964–15/02/1964

Despite this early indication that the TARDIS was something more, the Doctor continued to think of his ship as just an incredibly complex machine. His understanding of it deepened, however, during his third incarnation, when he all but totally dismantled the TARDIS and put it all back together again. Around this time, he began to refer to it as 'she' or 'old girl', making occasional comments about journey times depending on 'her mood', and once describing it as 'a living thing with thousands of instruments'. The ship itself provided the proof of this when the Third Doctor, approaching regeneration, got lost in the Vortex, and eventually the TARDIS took over and returned him to UNIT HQ.

The Fourth Doctor returned his ship's affection, at times talking to the TARDIS as if it were a fellow traveller ('Take no notice, old girl'), a habit he kept up through his next few regenerations. 'What a sentimental old thing this TARDIS is,' noted the Eighth Doctor after witnessing the revival of Grace Holloway and Chang Lee, carefully timed to coincide with the closing of the Eye of Harmony and a brightening of the lights.

By the time the Ninth Doctor faced Blon Fel Fotch Pasameer-Day Slitheen in the control room, there was no longer any doubt. With the Time War behind them, the Doctor was now fully aware that his ship, grown not built, was a living thing: 'You've opened its soul,' he told the Slitheen as she stared through an open console panel right into the heart of the TARDIS and it granted her wish to start again. Soon afterwards, stranded on Earth and with the Doctor facing half a million Daleks in the far future, Rose Tyler tried to persuade the ship to help her get back to the Game Station. It did not cooperate, perhaps reluctant to disobey the Doctor's wishes, but Rose managed to open up the console again and absorb the transforming energy of the Time Vortex.

So the TARDIS is, somehow, alive and able to think and act independently of the Doctor. Just like the Doctor, it recognised the simple wrongness of Captain Jack Harkness's immortality, and it fled through time to the end of the universe trying to shake him off.

It also reacted violently when it sensed the possibility of the Doctor's daughter, careering through time and space to 61st-century Messaline.

Both the Doctor and his TARDIS are now the last of their kind, and they share an unbreakable bond. Without the Doctor, as a parallel Donna discovered, the TARDIS would simply give up and die.

With him, though, the TARDIS can do pretty much anything. The time machine trusts the Doctor, and the Doctor trusts the TARDIS. They've been travelling together for hundreds of years, from the Big Bang to the end of the universe. They've journeyed into other realities, surfed the Medusa Cascade, and watched Spitfires fly into battle against the Daleks. Through it all, the Time Lord and his obsolete machine have kept on going, regenerating several times, seeing companions come and go. But, for the Doctor and his TARDIS, the journey will never end.

BOOM TOWN
by Russell T Davies
Starring Christopher Eccleston as the Doctor
First broadcast:
04/06/2005

UTOPIA
by Russell T Davies
Starring David Tennant as the Doctor
First broadcast:
16/06/2007

THE DOCTOR'S DAUGHTER
by Stephen Greenhorn
Starring David Tennant as the Doctor
First broadcast:
10/05/2008

TURN LEFT
by Russell T Davies
Starring David Tennant as the Doctor
First broadcast:
21/06/2008